A
PHILADELPHIA
STORY

EST. | 1682

Founders *and* Famous Families
from the City of Brotherly Love

A PHILADELPHIA STORY

EST. | 1682

Founders *and* Famous Families *from the* City of Brotherly Love

LORI LITCHMAN

CLERISY PRESS

A Philadelphia Story: Founders and Famous Families from the City of Brotherly Love

For further information, please contact the publisher:

 Clerisy Press
An imprint of AdventureKEEN
2204 1st Ave. S., Suite 102
Birmingham, AL 35233
clerisypress.com

Library of Congress Cataloging-in-Publication Data

Names: Litchman, Lori.
Title: A Philadelphia story : founders and famous families from the City of
    Brotherly Love / Lori Litchman.
Description: Covington, KY : Clerisy Press, 2016. | Includes bibliographical
    references and index.
Identifiers: LCCN 2015044042 | ISBN 9781578605699 (paperback)
    ISBN 9781578605705 (electronic)
Subjects: LCSH: Philadelphia (Pa.)—History. | Philadelphia (Pa.)—Biography.
    Statesmen—Pennsylvania—Philadelphia—Biography. | Families—
    Pennsylvania—Philadelphia—Biography. | Philadelphia (Pa.)—Social life
    and customs. | Historic sites—Pennsylvania—Philadelphia. | Historic
    buildiings—Pennsylvania—Philadelphia. | Philadelphia (Pa.)—Buildings,
    structures, etc. | BISAC: HISTORY / United States / State & Local / Middle
    Atlantic (DC, DE, MD, NJ, NY, PA).
Classification: LCC F158.3 .L78 2016 | DDC 974.8/11—dc23
LC record available at **lccn.loc.gov/2015044042**

Distributed by Publishers Group West
Printed in the United States of America
First edition, first printing

Project editor: Ritchey Halphen
Cover design: Scott McGrew
Text design: Annie Long and Travis Bryant
Cover photos: (*Front, top and bottom*) Ed Yakovich via Wikimedia Commons,
    public domain; unknown photographer, via Wikimedia Commons, public
    domain. (*Back, left*) Dave Tavani. (*Back, right*) *Penn's Treaty with the Indians*,
    by Benjamin West; via Wikimedia Commons, public domain.
Interior photos: As noted on page
Copyeditor: Lisa C. Bailey
Proofreader: Susan Elliott Brown
Indexer: Ann Weik Cassar / Cassar Technical Services

For my beloved city and all of her children

AUTHOR'S NOTE

Philadelphia is quite possibly my first true love.

I was not born here. I came to the city as a teenager when I attended a summer program at the University of Pennsylvania. I was a country bumpkin, having grown up in rural Pennsylvania. The city wooed me instantly with its immediacy of services and amenities, but it was the character of Philadelphia that hooked me. I grew up in a hardscrabble place, and Philadelphia had that same vibe. I could feel the love and work that went into the making of the city. I was head over heels in an instant.

I knew I had to go to college in Philadelphia. The following year, I started as a freshman at La Salle University, nestled in the Germantown section of the city. So began my decades-long love affair with Philadelphia. I truly love my city, and, as in any relationship, we have had our ups and downs. I actually wrote my MFA thesis about finding nature in Philadelphia, a feat that is easy to do, given the foundation of the city as William Penn's "greene countrie towne."

When offered the opportunity to write about Philadelphia's founders and famous families and their contributions to the city, I jumped at the chance. My research method included using what I already knew about Philadelphia and adding to that by spending a year researching and learning more. This book is not an academic text, nor is it your typical history book. I like to think of it as history for the modern reader: You can read it from start to finish, or you can flip around throughout to read short bits. It is a series of snapshots about the founders and families and how those people contributed to the firsts that helped make Philadelphia the city that it has become. And it is arranged thematically rather than chronologically, looking at how the city was shaped through areas like health, law, music, sports, and other facets of society.

I spent countless hours researching everything I could about the city and its people. Inevitably, I had to leave things out, else the book would end up a tome. Nevertheless, this is a work of nonfiction. Everything is real and fact-based.

As a resident of the city for decades, I'm keenly aware that Philadelphia is not without its problems—no major city is. However, I have consciously chosen not to emphasize political scandals, corruption, or other negative pieces of Philadelphia's history. You can find plenty about those things on your own. Rather, this book is meant to be a love story, because in times of love, the city has shone brightly. And as the city undergoes a renaissance, it's a great time to be a Philadelphian and to visit the birthplace of our nation. I hope that you find Philadelphia as charming as I do—and that you fall in love with her, too.

—*Lori Litchman*

CONTENTS

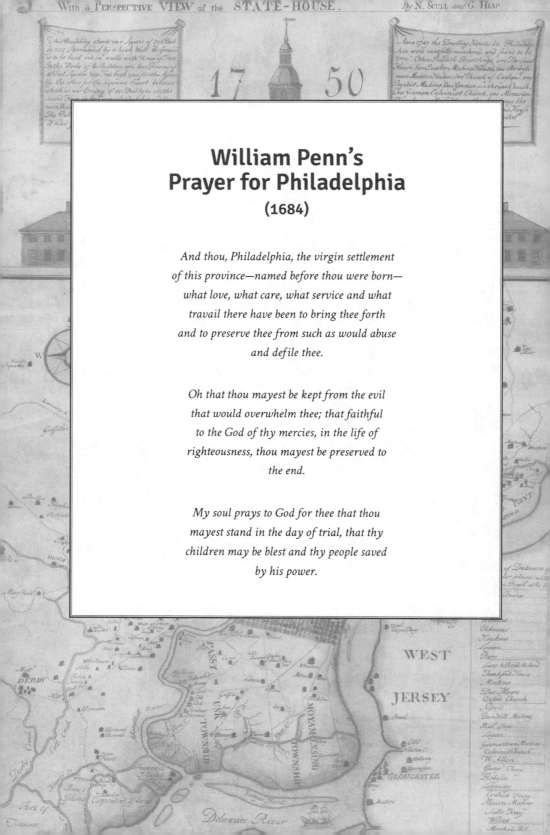

William Penn's Prayer for Philadelphia
(1684)

And thou, Philadelphia, the virgin settlement
of this province—named before thou were born—
what love, what care, what service and what
travail there have been to bring thee forth
and to preserve thee from such as would abuse
and defile thee.

Oh that thou mayest be kept from the evil
that would overwhelm thee; that faithful
to the God of thy mercies, in the life of
righteousness, thou mayest be preserved to
the end.

My soul prays to God for thee that thou
mayest stand in the day of trial, that thy
children may be blest and thy people saved
by his power.

INTRODUCTION

THE STORY OF THE CITY OF PHILADELPHIA is a love story. "How's that?" you might ask.

If you are a native Philadelphian or have lived in the city a long time, you totally know what I mean when I say that Philadelphia is all about love. You actually can feel that love every time you go out of town and return to see the skyline of our fair city glistening in the evening sunset. You can feel the warmth of the city when you walk along Kelly Drive and see fellow citizens out enjoying the day walking, biking, or running along the banks of the Schuylkill River. And you certainly feel a tinge of pride when you pass by historic Old City and witness throngs of visitors who have come to see where our nation was born.

If you are a visitor, however, you might think that Philadelphians, particularly Philadelphia sports fans, are a little harsh. You've probably heard the stories of sports fans going crazy and often even booing their own players. Philadelphians are nothing if not passionate—particularly about their sports teams. It's really just a family affair. Philadelphians love their sports teams so much they feel they can trash the players and teams one minute and embrace them the next—just like you might do to your annoying little brother. You can trash him all you want, but no one else better say a bad word about your brother in your presence. We are fiercely protective of our city. Yo, you got a problem with that?

When you learn about Philadelphia's history, you will realize that we are a scrappy city and, like any great American metropolis, we've had our ups and downs. But even when the city is down, it fights like hell to get back up. Because we love our city, warts and all.

Philadelphia's founder, William Penn, started the love train back in 1644. He wanted to create a utopian society where people could practice the religion of their choice without fear of persecution. He called his beloved city Philadelphia, Greek for "City of Brotherly Love." And people came in droves to live freely: By the time the first census was taken in 1790, Philadelphia proper—the area today known as Center City—boasted a population of more than 28,000 people.

But the population was not solely concentrated in the center of town. There were other municipalities nearby. In fact, early census data shows that Southwark, Northern Liberties, and Spring Garden were among the top 10 most populous places. However, the Act of Consolidation in 1854 unified all of those municipalities under the umbrella of Philadelphia, making the County of Philadelphia and the City of Philadelphia one and the same. By 1850, Philadelphia's population had climbed to more than 121,000, but consolidation expanded it to more than 500,000.

From its earliest manifestation, Philadelphia has always been a city of neighborhoods. Even though the Act of Consolidation technically unified all of Philadelphia County, neighborhoods retained their own character and still do to this day. Granted, neighborhoods have undergone changes throughout the years, but each of the more than 100 neighborhoods in Philadelphia has its own personality and traditions.

The first Philadelphians brought with them a love of innovation and a love of money. The "perennial Philadelphians," as they have

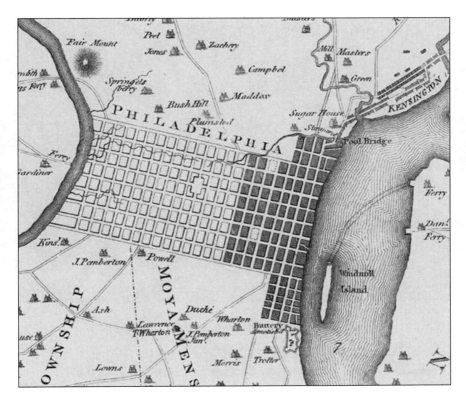

Philadelphia and nearby areas, 1777

Engraving by Will Faden; via Wikimedia Commons, public domain

come to be known, were the movers and shakers of Philadelphia. The founders of the city helped create a government for our nation that would emerge from the confines of Independence Hall. The Declaration of Independence and the US Constitution were both penned in Philadelphia, establishing the foundation for our country's freedom and democratic government.

The first families of the city created lasting legacies in nearly every facet of society, making Philadelphia a "city of firsts." From the first hospital to the first biomedical research facility, Philadelphia established itself as the bedrock of our country's medical community. To

A historical engraving of the Fairmount Water Works, circa 1835
(see Chapter 2)

(Engraving by W. H. Bartlett, published by J. C. Armytage; via Wikimedia Commons, public domain)

this day, Philadelphia is a vital medical education and research city. Philadelphia also set the standard for water cleanliness and delivery, being the first city to create a municipal water system that piped clean water throughout the city. And before Wall Street was the center of the financial universe, Philadelphia established the First Bank of the United States and was seen as the "cradle of American finance."

The founders and first families also established the standards for law and order for the nation. Before Washington, D.C., Philadelphia was the first capital city of the United States. Lawyers were common among the first Philadelphians, and the term "Philadelphia lawyer" was coined in reference to Andrew Hamilton's legal maneuverings while defending John Peter Zenger in a landmark freedom-of-the-press case. Today, "Philadelphia lawyer" is defined in *Merriam-Webster's*

Collegiate Dictionary as "a lawyer knowledgeable in the most minute aspects of the law."

As Philadelphia continued to grow in population and industry took over the country during the Industrial Revolution, the city remained a hub of innovation, adopting the moniker "Workshop of the World." From false teeth to toys and steel, Philadelphia was a manufacturing mecca. The city also became a textile empire, and factories reigned supreme across the city.

African Americans also have a deep-rooted history in Philadelphia. Because of Philadelphia's geographic location, the city became a major stop on the Underground Railroad as blacks journeyed toward their freedom. Prominent Quaker abolitionists aided freed African Americans and spoke out about the evils of slavery. In turn, African Americans established homes and communities in Philadelphia.

Penn's initial plan for Philadelphia was that every property would have green space. It's not that he was a nature nerd—he actually thought that having green space would help prevent fires. Penn saw his Philadelphia as a "greene countrie towne." From its earliest days, Philadelphia was verdant and still boasts the largest city park system in the country: Fairmount Park. Back in the day, scientists and naturalists abounded across the city, and their love of discovery established Philadelphia as a center for the natural sciences.

Throughout Philadelphia's early years, the city was also bursting with creative arts, boasting some of America's finest painters. In later history, Philadelphia became a prominent publishing center, home to such legendary publications as *Ladies' Home Journal* and *The Saturday Evening Post.*

What would Philadelphia be without its sports legends? From tennis superstars to a rowing Olympian to the famous Connie Mack, Philadelphians can play a good game. Long overshadowed by the "curse of William Penn," Philadelphia sports teams were ecstatic when the Phillies broke the curse in 2008 by winning the World Series. Today, Philadelphia's most famous fictional sports legend, Rocky Balboa, stands proudly at the foot of the steps of the Philadelphia Museum of Art, where tourists line up daily to get a photo with the boxing champ.

Philadelphians have always known how to have a good time. To this day, Philadelphians love a good drink, and there's history to support that. Philly was once the beer capital of the world, with hundreds of breweries throughout the town. Philly knows how to break it down, too. Philadelphia is home to music greats Kenny Gamble and Leon Huff, creators of the "Sound of Philadelphia," which included artists such as the O'Jays ("Love Train"). *American Bandstand,* created and filmed on location in Philadelphia, gave teenyboppers from across the city the opportunity to show off their moves on national television.

This book is by no means a comprehensive account of all of the founders, families, and firsts in Philadelphia. Rather, this book provides snapshots of the people whose legends linger in every nook and cranny of the city. It examines the founders and families of Philadelphia and how their stories and love of the city contributed to several segments of society, both locally and nationally. Often that love of innovation and discovery led to Philadelphia's becoming a city of firsts. This book is the story of Philadelphia's character. It's a tale of place, told through the stories of the people who loved it so much. It's a love story. So hop on the love train and enjoy the ride.

—*L. L.*

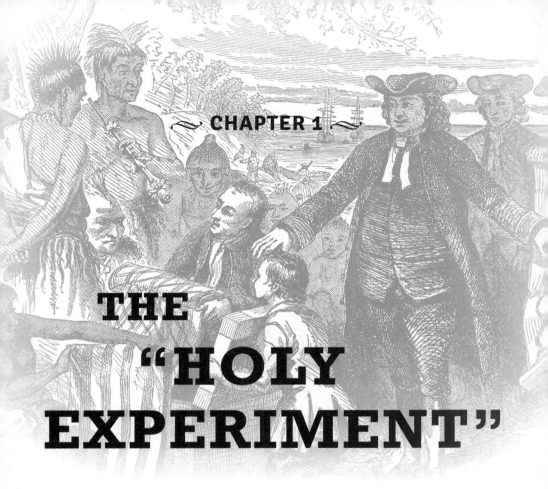

~ CHAPTER 1 ~

THE "HOLY EXPERIMENT"

WILLIAM PENN WATCHES OVER PHILADELPHIA DAILY. From high atop Philadelphia's City Hall, his countenance gazes peacefully over his beloved city, his "greene countrie towne," his City of Brotherly Love. When sports teams do well, William Penn celebrates by donning the jersey or hat of the winning team. But don't make him mad, or he'll curse the city and its sports teams.

Penn might be, quite arguably, the most well-known founder of an American city. Ask anyone to tell you who founded Chicago, Boston, or even New York City. Chances are the answer will not come anywhere nearly as quickly as it does in response to the question of who founded Philadelphia. Although Penn didn't spend very much time in his adopted home, his influence is everywhere—from the city's structure to the laws that govern our nation.

A Monumental Presence

High atop Philadelphia's City Hall stands the statue of William Penn. Weighing in at 27 tons of bronze, this 37-foot-tall presence can't be missed. City Hall was the tallest building in the world from 1901 to 1909, and for decades, not a single building rose above the hat of Philly's founder.

Penn stands proudly above his city, holding Pennsylvania's charter in his left hand. After a display of two years in City Hall's courtyard, Penn was lifted up to his final perch.

Sculptor Alexander Milne Calder designed the statue. He intended the sculpture to face south so the sun would naturally light the statue for most of the day. However, one of the building's architects decided that Penn should face to the northeast. There are several theories as to why. Some say he is facing Penn Treaty Park—the location of his treaty with the Native Americans. Others say he is facing his country home, Pennsbury Manor, in Bucks County. Regardless, Penn has been overseeing his city since 1894.

Alexander Milne Calder's statue of William Penn before it moved to the top of City Hall

(Photo: The British Library via Wikimedia Commons, public domain)

William Penn at age 22

(Painting attributed to Sir Peter Lely; via Wikimedia Commons, public domain)

The story of the founding of Pennsylvania, and ultimately Philadelphia, began thousands of miles away in England. King Charles II owed Penn's father, Admiral Sir William Penn, a great debt for his participation in the English Civil War. Philadelphia's William was the only son of the admiral, and early in life, the younger Penn was a rebel, causing his father great concern. After Penn was kicked out of Oxford, his father sent him packing.

In his early 20s, the younger William joined a fanatical religious group that was causing a ruckus throughout the United Kingdom. Members of the Religious Society of Friends were often subject to hangings and imprisonment. In 1680, Penn petitioned the king to request a colony in America between New York and Maryland. Penn wanted a place where he and his fellow Quakers could live without fear of persecution. The king saw the granting of Penn's request as a good way to settle the debt the crown owed Admiral Penn, who was dead at that point. The king gave the younger Penn 45,000 square miles of land, which Penn hoped to call New Wales. The king rejected Penn's choice for a name, so Penn came up with the name Sylvania (Latin for "woodsy place"). The king liked it, but he insisted Penn's name be attached to it as well, in honor of the senior William. So the new colony would be called Pennsylvania. As his Quaker faith emphasized personal humility, Penn tried (to no avail) to remove his name from his new colony because he didn't want his friends to think he was vain.

Penn received the king's charter in 1681, which stated that Penn would pay the crown "rent" each year in the form of two beaver skins. Penn also promised to give the king 20 percent of any silver or gold found in the new colony, which would eventually amount to nothing. Penn saw Pennsylvania as his "Holy Experiment" and believed his colony would be a place where people could embrace their Quaker ideals.

The king allowed Penn to name his capital city, and so he did. He named it Philadelphia, Greek for "City of Brotherly Love." He landed in New Castle, Delaware, on October 27, 1682, and headed to his new home.

Brotherly Love

EVEN THOUGH THE KING GAVE PENN THE LAND that became Pennsylvania, Penn was fully aware that native peoples had long been living there. He believed that he needed to pay the local Lenni Lenape tribe what he thought was a fair price for the land. Legend has it that in 1682, Penn paid the natives 1,200 pounds and signed a treaty with them under an elm tree at Shackamaxon, which is in the current neighborhood of Kensington. Rather than trying to forcefully take property, Penn decided to purchase a large riverfront parcel from the Swedes.

Penn chose not to have a military presence in Pennsylvania, which was quite uncommon for settlements at the time. He also refused

In the Spirit: Religious Life

PENN'S UTOPIAN SOCIETY, which guaranteed freedom of religion, did not have the same connotation of freedom that most people think of today: Although people could worship freely, only Christians were allowed to vote and hold office. Most Jews chose to worship in private homes until 1740, when Congregation Mikveh Israel was established. Catholics were barred also from holding office because Penn feared they would rely too heavily on the Pope's mandates. Regardless, people came in droves to worship in Pennsylvania. By the time of Penn's death in 1718, numerous religious communities had been established across the city.

- **Lutheran:** 142
- **Presbyterian:** 112
- **Mennonite:** 64
- **Anglican/Episcopalian:** 24
- **Roman Catholic:** 11
- **Jewish:** 2
- **German Reformed:** 126
- **Quaker:** 64
- **Baptist:** 24
- **Moravian:** 13
- **Methodist:** 7

Source: William C. Kashatus,
"William Penn's Legacy: Religious and Spiritual Diversity,"
Pennsylvania Heritage 38, no. 2 (2011).

to build a wall around his new city, instead wanting to befriend the native people. He even created a trial system so that if any European committed a crime against a native person, he/she would have a trial before an equal number of Europeans and native people.

Painter Benjamin West's take on Penn's treaty with the Lenni Lenape

(Via Wikimedia Commons, public domain)

One of Penn's greatest contributions to both his growing colony and an infant nation came in the form of a democratic system of government, elements of which would find their way into the foundational documents of the United States. He saw the incorporation of this system of government into his new colony as part of God's plan for humanity. He gave all men—but not slaves or women—the right to vote. At the time, England allowed only property owners to vote, so Penn certainly increased citizen participation, but voting rights for African Americans and women would come at a much later point in history.

Penn went on to create and implement the Charter of Privileges in October 1701. This charter was a constitution for Penn's colony that would later help lay the groundwork for the government of the United States. One of the key features of the charter was the creation of an assembly that could create bills, instead of merely accepting or rejecting bills from the governor and his council. The charter also included the election of representatives and a separation of powers.

The Charter of Privileges would remain the law of the land in Pennsylvania until the dawn of the Revolutionary War in 1776. To celebrate the charter's 50th anniversary, a bell was created in 1751 to mark the occasion. The bell weighed 2,080 pounds and was cast of copper. The following words were inscribed on the bell: PROCLAIM LIBERTY THROUGHOUT THE LAND UNTO ALL THE INHABITANTS THEREOF. That bell became known as the Liberty Bell and is housed at Independence National Historical Park, located in today's neighborhood of Old City.

The Liberty Bell with Independence Hall in the background

(Photo: Dave Tavani)

Equality was vital to Penn's Holy Experiment, and he ensured that people could freely practice whatever religion they chose. Many people who came to Pennsylvania were fleeing an inhospitable religious environment in Europe. And even though women could not vote, Penn saw equal education an imperative element to his society and provided schooling to both boys and girls.

The Grid System Is Born

HAVING LIVED IN LONDON and seen the destruction that disease and fire could wreak on a city, Penn wanted his city to be safe. He hired Captain Thomas Holme to be his surveyor, and after scouting out the territory, Holme chose to lay out the city about a mile from the

Delaware River, from today's South Street to Vine Street. According to historian Russell Frank Weigley, the area was a hardwood forest covered in oak, black walnut, chestnut, cypress, hickory, beech, and elm. When Penn arrived, however, he felt that the area Holme had chosen was too small, so Penn moved his city westward. Penn decided that his Philadelphia should be situated between the Delaware and the Schuylkill Rivers, so he bought a mile of land along the Schuylkill. Philadelphia would be a total of 1,200 acres and would be 1 mile wide and 2 miles long.

Penn's early vision for his "greene countrie towne" was to create large swaths of land for each purchaser. He imagined that each property would contain "gardens, orchards, and fields" and would be 800 feet apart from the neighboring lot. In his revised plan in 1682, Penn created somewhat smaller lots and laid them out in a rectangle. He reserved parcels of land to the north and west of Philadelphia (today's North and

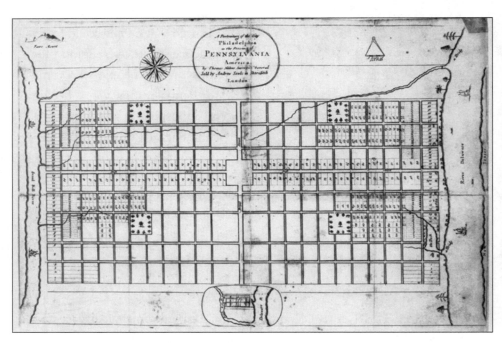

Thomas Holme's original layout of Philadelphia, 1683

West Philadelphia) and called those areas "liberty lands." Penn originally intended to build a home for himself in today's Fairmount section of the city, overlooking the Schuylkill River, but he would later decide to build his homestead, Pennsbury Manor, in what is now Bucks County.

Holme drew up Penn's plan, which would later become known as a grid system. Both High Street (today's Market Street) and Broad Street would be 100 feet wide and intersected by east–west running streets. Penn named those streets after trees: Cedar (today's South Street), Pine, Spruce, Walnut, Chestnut, Mulberry (today's Arch Street), Sassafras (today's Race Street), and Vine. The north–south streets were numbered, as they remain today.

Penn also created space for four sections of land that would be designated as park space open to the public. Today, those parks are known as Franklin Square, Logan Circle, Rittenhouse Square, and Washington Square. Penn designated the home of the city's current City Hall as the center of town and home to the Quaker meetinghouse, school, market, and state center. With that, the grid system for cities was born, and as urban areas developed across the country, they would often use Penn's system as a blueprint.

Short Stay

PENN'S FIRST STAY IN THE NEW WORLD was a short one, lasting less than two years. After acquiring Pennsylvania, Penn would spend a great deal of time battling with Lord Baltimore over boundaries. Lord Baltimore claimed that the southern portion of the state—which would have included Philadelphia—belonged to him. Penn met with Lord Baltimore in 1683 to try to settle the dispute of the southern border of the state, with no luck. In 1684, Penn received word that Lord Baltimore was headed back to England to try to establish the southern line of Pennsylvania, so Penn hopped on a boat and headed back to England to fight for his interests against Lord Baltimore. Penn was able to block a transfer of Pennsylvania's land to Maryland, but he wasn't able to get the crown to make a decision with regard to

Rittenhouse Square was one of Philadelphia's original town squares.

the southern border. In fact, the dispute over the southern border of Pennsylvania was not solved in Penn's lifetime, but rather with the drawing of the Mason-Dixon Line in 1763.

During his lifetime, Penn would have two wives and numerous children. His first wife, Gulielma Springett, died before she could make the journey overseas to visit her husband's colony. She and Penn had eight children, three of whom survived childhood: Laetitia, Springett, and William Jr. Two years after Gulielma's death in 1694, Penn married Hannah Callowhill, who was 25 years his junior. Together they had eight children, five of whom survived to adulthood: John, Thomas, Margaret, Richard, and Dennis. Only one of those children, John, was born in the New World: Born in 1700, he was nicknamed "The American."

After securing his property interests in the dispute with Lord Baltimore, Penn returned to Philadelphia in December 1699 with his new wife. When he returned to the colony, he brought with him his secretary, James Logan, who would become an integral part of the growth of Philadelphia and Pennsylvania. During this visit, Penn chose to stay in his country home, Pennsbury Manor. Regardless of his views on freedom, Penn had slaves and allowed slavery in his colony and at his home. (Slavery came to Pennsylvania in the 1640s, thus it had already been established by the time that Penn arrived.) There isn't much documented about Penn's slaves, but several of them were named in the historical accounts of Pennsbury Manor, where they lived and served. The known names of Penn's slaves were Sam, Sue, Yaff, Jack, and Peter.

In 1701, Penn got word that the English Parliament was planning on reclaiming Pennsylvania, so he again boarded a ship and headed back to England to protect his land. He was able to keep Pennsylvania, but he had many financial troubles during the last years of his life. A friend he had entrusted to manage his money ended up stealing from him. Litigation followed and lasted for years before the matter was settled. Penn suffered from a stroke in 1712 and died on July 30, 1718. He was 73 years old and never had the opportunity to return to his

beloved Pennsylvania. Even though Penn died a pauper, he left his colony in the care of his sons, John, Thomas, Richard, and Dennis, who hung on to the land until the American Revolution.

During the Revolutionary War, John Penn sided with the American cause. However, the Penn family lost its proprietorship over all of their land and were prohibited from participating in the new government established after the

James Logan, Penn's right-hand man

(Unknown artist; via Wikimedia Commons, public domain)

Leading Ladies:
Hannah Callowhill Penn

HANNAH CALLOWHILL PENN was William Penn's second wife. The two tied the knot in 1696, two years after the death of Penn's first wife, Gulielma Maria Springett. Hannah was 26 when she arrived in Philadelphia with her husband in December 1699. She was pregnant with the couple's first child, named John and always referred to as "The American." She and Penn had eight children together, three of whom died as infants.

Hannah Penn, second wife of William Penn and first woman governor of Pennsylvania

(Unknown artist; via Wikimedia Commons, public domain)

It was Hannah Penn's ability to manage affairs that became her legacy. In 1712, William Penn became incapacitated by a stroke, making his wife the acting proprietor of Pennsylvania. Hannah managed Pennsylvania from across the Atlantic until her death in 1726. She worked closely with James Logan, Penn's right-hand man, to help her.

After William Penn died in 1718, Hannah successfully dealt with her husband's debt, managed his estate, and settled a land dispute with Maryland. Hannah also battled with Penn's surviving children from his first wife and ensured that her three sons, John, Thomas, and Richard, would inherit Pennsylvania.

In 2014, then-Governor Tom Corbett said it was time to correct history and acknowledge Hannah as Pennsylvania's first female governor. A portrait of Hannah was commissioned to accompany the portraits of Pennsylvania's other governors.

separation from England. The Commonwealth of Pennsylvania paid John, his brother Richard, and a cousin 130,000 pounds. The Penn family was able to hold onto several thousand acres of land across Pennsylvania that were passed down for several generations.

When Penn received his charter from the king in 1681, there were only a few hundred people living in the area now known as Philadelphia. By the time of his death, that number had exploded into the thousands. Penn's "Holy Experiment" would also greatly influence the development of the government of the United States, and Philadelphia would serve as the home base and capital city for years to come.

> **PHILLY FACT** In 1984, during the Reagan administration, an Act of Congress declared William Penn and his second wife, Hannah Callowhill Penn, honorary American citizens.

~ CHAPTER 2 ~

TO YOUR HEALTH

A S PHILADELPHIA'S POPULATION CONTINUED TO GROW, two
separate classes were beginning to form: the elite class and the
artisan class. A rhyme was even devised to help people remember
all the members of the elite class: "Morris, Norris, Rush and Chew /
Drinker, Dallas, Coxe and Pugh / Wharton, Pepper, Pennypacker /
Willing, Shippen and Markoe." By 1730, the population of Penn's city
was around 11,500. Out of that artisan class came Benjamin Franklin,
a humble printer who moved to Philadelphia from Boston and would
ultimately become better known than Penn and become involved in
nearly every facet of colonial society. Arguably, without Ben Franklin
and his ability to make friends and influence people, Philadelphia
would be without numerous firsts, including a number of health

initiatives that would shape the culture of medicine and health care in early America and for generations to come.

Mr. Philadelphia

FRANKLIN WAS BORN IN 1706 IN BOSTON, came to Philadelphia as a teenager in 1723, and loved the city so much that he stayed. Throughout his life, he would become not only an iconic Philadelphian but also a founding father of the country and poster boy for the self-made man living the American dream. Franklin is best known as one of the authors of the Declaration of Independence and led a notable life as a politician and a statesman. He was a printer and publisher by trade; he owned the *Pennsylvania Gazette* newspaper and garnered recognition for his publication of *Poor Richard's Almanack*. He later became immersed in the sciences. One of his first inventions was the Franklin stove, a wood stove that was more efficient than the open fireplaces of the time period. Then later in life when his eyesight was failing, Franklin invented the bifocal lens.

> **PHILLY FACT** "Beer is proof that God loves us and wants us to be happy." This quote is often attributed to Mr. Philadelphia himself, Ben Franklin, regarding his fondness for a good brew. Unfortunately, there is no documentation that he ever said it, and the evidence actually points to him favoring wine.

He was a voracious reader and wanted to share his love of books with his fellow Philadelphians, which helped facilitate the creation of the first lending library—The Library Company of Philadelphia. Thomas Cadwalader was also one of the founders of the Library Company. Franklin had previously gathered a group of like-minded men to meet on Friday nights to imbibe and discuss politics, morals, and science. The group was called the Junto (from the Spanish word for "together"), and together the men birthed The Library Company of Philadelphia. Back then, books were incredibly expensive, and only the elite could afford to have a large library. Franklin came up with an idea for the members of the Junto to gather their friends and ask all of them to share their collective wealth. Franklin asked 50 subscribers

Benjamin Franklin, a Philadelphia original

(Painting by Joseph-Siffrein Duplessis; via Wikimedia Commons, public domain)

to donate 40 shillings each and commit to an annual donation of 10 shillings a year for the next 50 years. Penn's secretary, James Logan, considered the "best judge of books in these parts," helped pick out the first books to buy for the library. Logan himself had an enormous collection of books—4,000 of which his descendants bequeathed to the Library Company in 1795. The Library Company of Philadelphia exists today as an independent research library that is free and open to the public and specializes in American history and culture from the 17th through 19th centuries.

The Junto eventually became the wellspring of another scientific organization—the American Philosophical Society. In 1739, Philadelphia botanist John Bartram came up with the idea of starting a Junto-like club of "the most ingenious and curious men" who would gather together to discuss science. Bartram was not the people person that Franklin was, so he turned to his friend to help him gather support for the club. Franklin started the buzz for the proposed academy of "learned" men, and in May 1743, the American Philosophical Society (APS) was born. Many of the country's founding fathers ultimately became members, including George Washington, John Adams, Thomas Jefferson, and Alexander Hamilton. Today, the APS is a museum open to the public that houses a collection of Franklin's personal books, the journals of Lewis and Clark, and 800 letters from Charles Darwin.

In addition to his noble and scientific pursuits, Franklin was a key figure in numerous practical advances in early Philadelphia society that ultimately made the city safer and more livable. One of those developments was Franklin's role in the creation of fire companies and insurance. Concerned over the city's ability to fight fires, Franklin published his concerns in his newspaper and discussed them with the members of the Junto. In December 1736, Franklin and a group of 30 men launched the Union Fire Company. Their firefighting equipment, which consisted of leather buckets and "strong bags," was primitive by today's standards. But in a short matter of time, Philadelphians banded together to form several other volunteer fire companies. Knowing that these companies would not prevent or even stop all fires, Franklin and members of the Union Fire Company met with other fire companies, and together they created the country's first property insurance company: The Philadelphia Contributionship for the Insuring of Houses from Loss by Fire. Subscribers would pay a fee each year and be able to recover their losses should a fire damage their home. Today, The Philadelphia Contributionship Mutual Holding Company is still insuring Philadelphians and also operates Vector Security Holdings, which offers a variety of security systems.

One of the most famous stories about Franklin is the one everyone learns as a kid. The story goes something like this: It was a dark and stormy night when the founding father decided to harness the power of lightning by concocting a silk kite with a metal key placed in a Leiden jar, an early tool for storing electricity. Franklin believed that if lightning was indeed electricity, he would be able to capture said energy in the jar by way of the key.

Allegedly, Franklin flew his kite, which was obviously struck by lightning. When he moved his hand toward the key in the jar, he was shocked, literally, to discover his hypothesis was correct. Throughout the years, though, scientists and historians believed the story to be complete rubbish because, if it were true, Franklin would have most certainly died from the charge. In fact, the Discovery Channel show *MythBusters* set out to prove the story a fraud. They suited up a gel dummy and attached a silk kite and key to it. They also outfitted the fake Franklin with a monitor to determine how much electricity would have gone into his body. The experiment showed that Franklin would have fried if it were true, effectively debunking the kite-and-key legend.

Chances are that Franklin wrote about such an experiment in his newspaper but, knowing that such a successful experiment could kill him, he didn't actually conduct it. Some also suggest that Franklin may have flown a kite before the storm hit and was able to collect a small amount of electricity to prove that his theory that lightning was in fact electricity was true. Franklin later invented the lightning rod, a key component in helping prevent fires in colonial America and still to this day.

The development of Philadelphia as an educational hub is also grounded in the contributions Franklin made to his adopted city. Franklin wanted the youth of Pennsylvania to get educated there and not need to go to another colony or Europe. He wanted to create a nonsectarian college where students could prepare to be government and business leaders. They would study the sciences and would be taught in English rather than Greek or Latin. Franklin first started two schools for younger children—The Academy and the Charity School of Philadelphia—with the hopes of preparing students there for higher education. In 1755, Franklin and a board of trustees were granted a charter for the College of Philadelphia. The College of Philadelphia later combined with the University of the State of Pennsylvania, which became known what is today as the University of Pennsylvania. In 1765, the school founded the nation's first medical school. Dr. John Morgan, who earned his medical degree at the University of Edinburgh, is credited with founding the medical school. Morgan was also a founding member of the American Philosophical Society and a doctor at Pennsylvania Hospital. Morgan, along with William Shippen, led many of the first lectures at Penn's new medical school. Shippen helped found Penn and Princeton (formerly the College of New Jersey), was an original member and vice president of the American Philosophical Society, and served on the Continental Congress.

Med Men

FRANKLIN'S ABILITY TO PULL TOGETHER the best and brightest in Philadelphia is ultimately what led to a cleaner, healthier Philadelphia. One of Franklin's greatest contributions to both Philadelphia and American society was the support and leverage he put behind starting the nation's first hospital. As Philadelphia's population continued to balloon, so did the need for care for the "sick-poor and insane who were wandering the streets of Philadelphia." In the early 18th century, Penn's city was the fastest growing of all the 13 colonies. One of Franklin's friends, Dr. Thomas Bond, came up with the idea to start a hospital in Philadelphia. Bond, a native of Maryland, had worked with Franklin on many of his projects, including the Library Company and the American Philosophical Society. Bond studied medicine in London and spent some time in France at a time when the idea of hospitals was emerging.

The original building of Pennsylvania Hospital, the country's first hospital

In 1750, Bond came up with the notion of building a hospital in Philadelphia, a new idea for the developing city and nation. As the story goes, when Bond asked Philadelphians to support the idea, many asked what Franklin thought of it. So Bond approached his friend, who immediately gave his support for the hospital. In fact, Franklin created what may have been the first American fundraising plan. Franklin went to the Pennsylvania Assembly and told them that he would raise 2,000 pounds from the general public to support the hospital, and if he could garner such support, then the Assembly should match the funds. The General Assembly thought that Franklin would fail, but he ended up raising more than 2,000 pounds, and the General Assembly gave the green light for the hospital in 1751. The hospital purchased land from the Penn family in 1754, and the doors to the new building at Eighth and Pine Streets opened in 1756, where the building still stands. Today it is referred to as the Pine Building and remains open. Bond shared his knowledge of medicine by giving lectures, which were offered to the first students at Penn's new medical school at the hospital. Bond earned the moniker "The Father of Clinical Medicine." He spent the rest of his life working at the hospital until his death in 1784. Bond's brother, Phineas, also aided his brother in the hospital's founding and was one of the first doctors to serve at the hospital. Today, Pennsylvania Hospital is affiliated with the University of Pennsylvania. Philadelphia also serves as a major medical hub in the United States, home to five medical schools within the city limits.

One of the most important (and controversial) doctors to come out of Pennsylvania Hospital was Dr. Benjamin Rush, dubbed "The Father of American Psychiatry" for his dedication to treating the mentally ill. Rush is also well known for his use of bloodletting to cure patients, particularly those with yellow fever during the two epidemics Philadelphia experienced. He was a signer of the Declaration of Independence and kept the company of other founding fathers, including John Adams, Thomas Jefferson, and Thomas Paine. He was a tireless advocate for the poor, the mentally ill, slaves, and women. He helped found the first antislavery organization in the colonies—the Pennsylvania Society for Promoting the Abolition of Slavery and the Relief of Free Negroes Unlawfully Held in Bondage. He also created the Philadelphia Dispensary, which provided medical care to the poor of Philadelphia, the first facility of its kind in the developing nation.

Rush was born outside of Philadelphia in 1746 and attended the College of New Jersey, known today as Princeton University.

Portrait of Benjamin Rush
by Charles Willson Peale

(Via Wikimedia Commons, public domain)

Museum of Medical Oddities

HAVE YOU EVER WONDERED what Einstein's brain was like? Well, you can see for yourself—literally—at the **Mütter Museum** of The College of Physicians of Philadelphia. Surgeon Thomas Dent Mütter donated 1,700 objects and $30,000 to the college. His mission was to reform medical education, and he made the college promise to "hire a curator, maintain and expand the collection, fund annual lectures, and erect a fireproof building."

The museum's first location was at 13th and Locust Streets and opened in 1863. Today, the museum is located at 19 S. 22nd St. and houses more than 25,000 objects. Some of the things you can see at the Mütter Museum include slides of Albert Einstein's brain, more than 5,500 historical medical instruments, hundreds of bones, and numerous body parts floating in jars.

After Rush earned his degree, his uncle encouraged him to study medicine rather than law. Rush found a mentor in Dr. John Redman and attended lectures at Penn's new medical school. Rush ultimately chose to go overseas to study medicine. At the same time, Franklin was overseas, and the two became friends. Rush was even elected to the American Philosophical Society before his return to Philadelphia. Upon his return to the city of brotherly love, Rush was appointed as chair of the College of Philadelphia's chemistry department. Rush was also one of 24 doctors to found the College of Physicians of Philadelphia in 1787, the country's first private medical organization. The founders said the organization's mission was "to advance the science of medicine and to thereby lessen human misery."

After the Revolutionary War, Rush added courses to his teaching load to include the practice of medicine. He was a beloved teacher, and by the end of his career, he had taught more than 3,000 medical students. He worked as a senior doctor at Pennsylvania Hospital for 30 years, and during that time, he instituted reforms for treatment of the mentally ill. He believed in treating patients with mental illness as human beings, and he abolished cruel practices and procedures that were established medicine. He published the first psychiatry textbook in America, *Medical Inquiries and Observations Upon the Diseases of the Mind,* in 1812, the year before he died of typhus fever. Rush was harshly criticized, however, for his treatment of yellow-fever patients during the epidemic Philadelphia experienced in 1793.

Fever Falls on Philadelphia

ONE OF THE MOST DEVASTATING BLOWS to Philadelphia's prosperity came in 1793 by way of a yellow-fever epidemic. At this point in time, Philadelphia was still the capital of both the state of Pennsylvania and the growing nation. The epidemic grew from a few cases of the infection along the Delaware waterfront and spread rapidly throughout the city. The population of the city was approximately 55,000, and everyone was terrified of the sickness. At the time, no one knew the cause of the disease or how it was spread. Panic set in, and tens of thousands of Philadelphians fled the city at the urging of Rush. Controversy arose about the suspected origin, with one camp (including Rush) convinced that the fever was born in Philadelphia, while the other side believed it came from foreigners entering the city. Rush was adamant that the sickness was due to the unsanitary conditions of the city, particularly the contamination of water from sewage and rotting food and coffee on the docks. One particularly disgusting part of the city was the area around today's Dock Street. Back then, Dock Creek flowed freely and became a dumping ground for waste from breweries, tanneries, and households.

The College of Physicians convened to discuss the matter and how best to treat people. Controversy arose about how to treat afflicted patients,

Dr. Philip Syng Physick,
"Father of American Surgery"

(Photo: Wmpearl via Wikimedia Commons, public domain)

with Rush adamant that blood-letting was the best way to purge the fever. He had a few supporters who agreed with his methods, but most medical professionals vehemently disagreed. The College of Physicians ultimately believed that the fever was contagious and originated overseas, in stark contrast to Rush's beliefs. Rush fell ill with yellow fever in September and followed his own treatment, recovering completely from the sickness. He was eventually forced to resign from the College of Physicians, and some even suggested that criminal charges be filed against him.

During this time, one of Rush's friends and colleagues, Dr. Philip Syng Physick, was helping treat yellow-fever victims. Physick himself came down with the illness and credited Rush's bloodletting treatment with his recovery. Physick studied medicine in Europe, where he learned the art of surgery. After the epidemic, Rush repaid Physick's support by referring surgical patients to his friend. Physick began seeing surgical patients in his private practice, and then joined Pennsylvania Hospital in 1794. He also became the first professor of surgery at Penn's medical school. He is widely considered the "Father of American Surgery," and his home in the Society Hill section of the city is now a museum.

We now know that yellow fever is a virus that is spread by mosquitoes, and epidemiologists believe it originated in Africa. There is no cure, but there is a preventive vaccine. Historians estimate the death toll from the Yellow Fever Epidemic of 1793 to be about 5,000. The virus and subsequent flight of Philadelphians had a crippling effect on the growth of the formerly burgeoning city. In fact, some historians cite the yellow-fever epidemic as one of the key events that allowed New York City to gain an edge over Philadelphia as the country was still developing. One positive development after the end of the health crisis was the city's creation of a Board of Health in 1794. The board oversaw health issues in the city for about 10 years before the city created a formal department of health in 1804, called the Department of Public Health and Charities.

Water, Water Everywhere

THE YELLOW FEVER EPIDEMIC OF 1793 also was the impetus for the city to clean up its water supply. Raw sewage was regularly discarded near drinking wells, and people suspected that these unsanitary conditions caused yellow fever. Another yellow-fever outbreak in 1798 hastened the public's outcry for clean water. Citizens petitioned the city to figure out a way to clean up the city's water supply, and by 1799, the city had formed a Watering Committee to address the issue. Adding another notch on its belt of firsts, Philadelphia became the first major city in the country and the world to take on the responsibility of supplying clean water to its populace.

Benjamin Henry Latrobe, considered to be one of the fathers of American architecture, happened to be in Philly during this time working on the building of the Bank of Philadelphia. The city asked Latrobe for his advice, and he said the best solution would be to tap the abundant water supply from the Schuylkill River and find a way to distribute the water to the city. He recommended the use of steam engines to power the system, even though the technology wasn't widely used at this time. His plan called for the building of two separate structures for the engines. The first building would be on Chestnut Street and would funnel the water through a tunnel to Broad Street, where

Benjamin Henry Latrobe, a father of American architecture

(Painting by Charles Willson Peale; via Wikimedia Commons, public domain)

the second structure, a pump house, would move the water to a reservoir at the top of the building. This structure was to be located at Centre Square, where City Hall sits today. The water would then use the force of gravity to find its way through hollowed-out logs to water subscribers. The Watering Committee loved the plan and gave Latrobe the contract to build the structure, which opened for business in January 1801.

The new water-supply system was a success, but it couldn't keep up with the demand in the growing city. It was also very costly to maintain and had its share of technical difficulties. Yellow fever reared its head again in the early 1800s, and the Watering Committee again looked for a solution to its water crisis. One of Latrobe's assistants, Frederick Graff, became the central figure in the construction of a new facility. Graff suggested that the new facility be located at "Faire Mount," the highest point in the city at the time. Graff was the superintendent of the waterworks at Centre Square and was greatly influenced by Latrobe's design there. Built in the Classical Revival style, the Fairmount Water Works opened for business in 1815. Not only was it ahead of its time in providing clean water to the population, but it was also an architectural marvel that became a popular tourist attraction. No trip to Philadelphia was complete without a visit there.

The Fairmount Water Works (shown here facing southeast, with the Philadelphia Museum of Art in the background) was an industrial and architectural marvel of its day.

(Photo: Historic American Buildings Survey, National Park Service; via Wikimedia Commons, public domain)

In 1819, the city decided to harness the power of the Schuylkill by building a dam across the expanse of the river. On July 23, 1821, the first drops of water spilled over the newly constructed dam, and a year later the Water Works transitioned from steam power to hydropower. Graff's design of the Fairmount Water Works became the prototype for water supplies across the growing nation. Latrobe's structure was eventually torn down in 1829.

Graff died in 1847, and his son, Frederick Graff Jr., took over as the superintendent of Fairmount Water Works. Graff Jr. saw a need to

From City Square to Boneyard and Back

WASHINGTON SQUARE IS A FAVORITE PLACE for Philadelphians and tourists to stroll through during any season to take in its pastoral beauty in the middle of the city. One of Penn's original squares, it was laid out in the plan of the city in 1682. Back then it was called Southeast Square.

However, within 25 years of the founding of Philadelphia, the square had become a potter's field—a cheap burial ground for the poor and unknown in the city. Later, during the Revolutionary War, deceased soldiers were buried in pits at the square. When the British took over Philadelphia in 1777, they kept prisoners of war in the Walnut Street Jail. Anyone who died in the prison ended up in the square. And—you guessed it—during the Yellow Fever Epidemic of 1793, the square became a massive grave site for those who succumbed to the sickness.

In 1815, the city decided to turn the 6.4-acre area back into a public park, planting trees and beautifying the space. The park was renamed Washington Square in 1825 in honor of George Washington.

Today, it serves as a public green space in the city and is a favorite resting area for lunching Philadelphians and visiting tourists. And no ghost tour is complete in the city without stopping by the square and talking about its storied history.

ensure the safety and cleanliness of the water supply for the city and pushed the city to acquire land along the banks of the Schuylkill River. The city started buying land in 1855 and continued to do so through 1890, effectively creating thousands of acres of a buffer zone that is known today as Fairmount Park. The Fairmount Park Commission was created in 1867, and Frederick Graff Jr. was one of the first commissioners of the new government body. Today, Fairmount Park covers more than 9,200 acres and is one of the largest urban parks in the world.

Medical Milestones

ANOTHER NOTABLE FIRST in Philadelphia's health history is the founding of the country's first independent biomedical research facility. The Wistar Institute opened its doors in 1892. The institute derives its name from Dr. Caspar Wistar, a prominent early doctor. Wistar, who started his medical practice in 1787, was the author of the first American textbook on anatomy. Wistar was friends with Thomas Jefferson and was a president of the American Philosophical Society. He was also a professor and chair at Penn's medical school in the Department of Anatomy. Throughout his career, Wistar would collect preserved human body parts, which he would dry and inject with wax. His friend, Rush, also constructed sculpted anatomical models. The collection kept growing in size and use and ultimately became known as the Wistar and Horner Museum, the second name originating from Wistar's friend Dr. William Edmonds Horner.

A fire in the University of Pennsylvania facility that housed the collection caused the provost at the time, Dr. William Pepper, to start a movement to provide a home for the collection where medical professionals could study. Wistar, whose family was widely involved in Philadelphia society, died in 1818. Some years later, his great-nephew, Isaac Jones Wistar, came to the rescue of the collection. Isaac Wistar was a prominent lawyer and brigadier general in the Civil War and decided to make a generous donation that led to the creation of The Wistar Institute of Anatomy and Biology. The Wistar Institute grew into a center for medical and biological research. It has been a leader in research in the areas of vaccines, cancer, DNA, gene expression, and numerous other areas.

Other notable medical firsts include the following:

- The nation's first children's hospital, **The Children's Hospital of Philadelphia (CHOP),** is known today as the Children's Hospital of the University of Pennsylvania. Dr. Francis West Lewis founded it in 1855, aided by two colleagues, Drs. T. Hewson Bache and R. A. F. Penrose.
- The nation's first eye hospital, **Wills Eye Hospital,** was established in 1832 by James Wills. Today it is part of Thomas Jefferson University.
- The nation's first medical school for women, **The Women's Medical College of Pennsylvania,** was founded in 1850. It was later renamed The Medical College of Pennsylvania in 1970 when men were admitted. It is now part of the Drexel University College of Medicine.
- **Friends Hospital** is the oldest private psychiatric hospital in the nation. Quakers founded it in 1813 to provide dignity and support for those suffering from mental illness. It still operates today in northeast Philadelphia.

End of an Era, Beginning of a Legacy

IN HIS PULITZER PRIZE–WINNING BIOGRAPHY, *Benjamin Franklin,* author Carl Van Doren wrote, "No other town burying its great man, ever buried more of itself than Philadelphia with Franklin." Franklin had had problems with his lungs for years when an abscess there finally burst, causing his death on April 17, 1790. He was buried four days later when an estimated 20,000 people (half of the city) attended his funeral. The nation mourned his loss. He is buried at Christ Church, where tourists can regularly visit his final resting place and toss pennies on his tombstone in the hopes that Franklin's spirit will give them good luck. Christ Church also plays its own role in the founding of the nation, as men as prestigious as Franklin worshiped there in the nation's infant years. It was founded in 1695, was the first Church of England parish in the colonies, and was the birthplace of the American Episcopal Church.

Franklin's name is ubiquitous in Philadelphia, with everything from streets to schools bearing it. In 1824, Samuel Vaughan Merrick, along with William Keating, founded The Franklin Institute of the

Leading Ladies: Deborah Read Franklin

IF THE SAYING "Behind every successful man is a woman" holds true, then Deborah Read Franklin was just as important to the nation's founding as her husband, Ben. Deborah's strong head for business enabled her husband to get so involved in politics.

Deborah Franklin, Mrs. Philadelphia

(Painting attributed to Benjamin Wilson; via Wikimedia Commons, public domain)

When Franklin first came to Philadelphia as a teenager, he stayed at the Read household, where he first met Deborah. The two became very close, and Deborah wanted to get married. Franklin, however, was sent to England on business. While he was overseas, Deborah's mother convinced her to marry another man, John Rogers. The marriage was an unhappy one and ended quickly. There were even rumors that Rogers had a wife in England.

When Franklin returned, he asked Deborah to marry him, but she worried that she would be accused of bigamy. So the two eventually entered into common-law marriage, living as husband and wife without ever formally marrying.

The couple had two children, one of whom died of smallpox as a toddler.

While Franklin involved himself in many aspects of Philadelphia society and national and international politics, Deborah quietly ran the couple's businesses, including a bookshop and a general store.

Deborah died of a stroke in 1774 while her husband was overseas. The two are buried next to each other at Christ Church Cemetery.

State of Pennsylvania for the Promotion of the Mechanic Arts, now known simply as The Franklin Institute. Merrick was a prominent businessman, and Keating was a scientist; they created the museum to honor Franklin. Philadelphia's love of Franklin is so strong that even during the Great Depression, The Franklin Institute, along with the Poor Richard Club, managed to raise $5.1 million dollars to build a new science museum. In 1932, The Franklin Institute opened the doors of its iconic stone building at the corner of 20th Street and the Benjamin Franklin Parkway. These days, thousands of schoolchildren delight in the hands-on activities in the museum each week.

In 2006, many of Franklin's living descendants gathered in Philadelphia to celebrate the 300th birthday of their famed relation. They met at the Christ Church Burial Ground to pay their respects. Historians estimate that Franklin has about 3,380 descendants, with about 2,000 of those alive today. Franklin's legacy lives on not only through his bloodline but also through the indelible mark he made on Philadelphia and the nation.

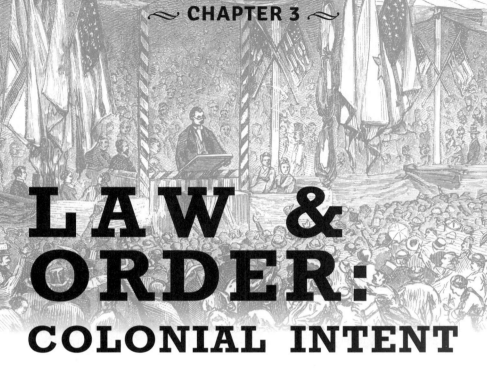

~ CHAPTER 3 ~

LAW & ORDER:
COLONIAL INTENT

URING THE EARLY DAYS OF PHILADELPHIA, there were "sacred
professions." Medicine was the first, with law taking second place.
According to Nathaniel Burt's classic book *The Perennial Philadelphians,*
society in early Philadelphia seemed to hold the profession of law in a
higher esteem than medicine. "Between the two, the law is more Solid,
medicine more Noble, and since Philadelphia on the whole prefers the
solid to the noble, law does perhaps have the edge."

It's impossible to talk about Philadelphia without addressing the role
the city played in the founding of our nation. Philadelphia is where the
country publicly decried the need to sever ties with the mother country, England. And the founding fathers created the nation's government structure in the City of Brotherly Love. Countless books, films,
and school courses have detailed the founding of the nation, but here's
a quick-and-dirty rehashing of the details surrounding the ultimate

creation of the US Constitution, because it is relevant to understanding what was going on in Philadelphia during its adolescent years.

Revolutionary Nation

IT'S KIND OF BOSTON'S FAULT that Philadelphia became ground zero during the rising tension between England and the colonies. Everyone on this side of the pond was angry with England's new tax laws. But things got real when Bostonians dumped more than 300 cases of tea into Boston Harbor. King George III tried to put the city in its place by stationing soldiers across Boston in private homes. Paul Revere got on a horse and headed to Philadelphia to try to get help and stop the same thing from happening in other parts of the colonies. Three hundred Philadelphians met up at a popular bar named City Tavern (more about this in Chapter 10) to discuss what to do with England. Ben Franklin had tried to gather a meeting of the minds previously, but it wasn't until the Boston Tea Party that the other power players agreed.

A few months after Revere came to Philadelphia, in September 1774, the First Continental Congress convened in Philadelphia to brainstorm about asking England to meet the demands of the colonies or deal with a boycott of anything coming from England. The founding fathers chose Philadelphia—and Pennsylvania—because of its "keystone" location. It was halfway for all the colonies to the north and south. At this time, the colonies really didn't want anything to do with war. Among other things, they just didn't want to have to pay taxes and have soldiers hanging around their houses. So the colonists figured if they asked nicely, then maybe England would agree. But then the bullets started to fly at Lexington and Concord, and the rest, as they say, is history. In May 1775, the Second Continental Congress met in Philadelphia. The Congress again asked England to settle down and leave the colonies alone.

But England wouldn't budge, and so the colonies decided that enough was enough. On July 4, 1776, the Declaration of Independence (which was penned in Independence Hall) passed, and the colonies officially declared their intent to break up with England. And just like that, the American Revolution was officially on, even though it had been brewing for some time.

The British saw capturing Philadelphia as key to winning the war. And it seemed that Philadelphia was a goner in late 1776, until George Washington came to the rescue Christmas night, famously crossing the Delaware River and snagging about 1,000 Hessians, who were fighting with the British. After two years of battles, of American wins and losses, the British finally hightailed it out of Philadelphia in 1778. In 1783, after negotiations to cease the war, the Treaty of Paris officially ended the war and recognized the United States as an independent nation. Ben Franklin was a member of the negotiating team, as were John Adams and John Jay.

Since you can't have a war without people to fight it, the Revolutionary War brought with it the birth of the US military. First came the army. Technically, the first soldiers were located in Massachusetts, but out of fear of getting whooped by the Brits, the loosely formed band of brothers contacted the Second Continental Congress in Philadelphia for help. It was during the spring of 1775 that legend has it that John Adams voted to take on the military that had created itself in Boston. There's no written account of this approval, but Congress moved swiftly thereafter to form a committee to oversee the creation of an army and approved $2 million in funding to support troops in Boston and New York City. Congress then authorized the creation of 10 more groups of soldiers who were sent to Boston to support the initial soldiers there. Next came the navy. On October 13, 1775, the Continental Congress approved a resolution to buy two armed ships. Within a few days, Congress created a Naval Committee, and later the first ships of the US Navy sailed from the port of Philadelphia. Finally, in November of the same year, a committee of the Continental Congress met up at a local watering hole, Tum Tavern, where they penned a resolution to create a marine corps that would battle both on land and sea. The resolution passed on November 10, and the US Marine Corps was born.

Pennsylvania was undergoing its own government building around this time. The state had adopted its own constitution in 1776 that was controversial and incredibly democratic. Framers of the federal constitution would look to the Pennsylvania document for guidance, to both adopt a similar structure and reject key elements of Pennsylvania's government. Although the makers of the US Constitution ultimately rejected much of Pennsylvania's structure, they embraced other elements that are still part of the constitution today. One such feature was the limit that the state constitution placed on the power of the legislature, namely that the legislature couldn't change the constitution. The state constitution was replaced in 1790 by one that included more checks and balances and more rights allotted to citizens.

The Constitutional Convention took place in Philadelphia. In May 1787, delegates from 12 states gathered again in Independence Hall to draft the structure of the newfound nation's governmental structure. By September, there was a final draft to present to the states. Delaware was the first to ratify the constitution, and by June of the following year, New Hampshire's signature was the tipping point, and the document became the law of the land.

After the Constitutional Convention, the new nation needed a capital city. In 1789, New York City was designated the temporary capital and is where the country's first president, George Washington, took his oath of office. New York, Philadelphia, and Virginia were all hopeful to become home to the nation's capital, but ultimately Washington, D.C., would win. Philadelphia served as home to the capital until the newer, better capital was built along the Potomac River. The hope was that once the government settled into Philadelphia, maybe it would decide to stay. At the time, Philadelphia was a world-class city, but that feeling of success and prosperity came crashing down in 1793 when the Yellow Fever Epidemic struck.

With the capital located in the city, there was great cause for concern about the well-being of the president and his cabinet members when the fever came. So they fled. They landed about 5 miles away in Germantown, which was not part of the city at that point in history.

Battle of the Bells

ST. MARK'S, a stately Episcopal church at 16th and Locust Streets, is located in what has long been an upscale neighborhood. St. Mark's was built in the 1850s but didn't have its bells installed until the 1870s. When they did start ringing regularly, the church's well-to-do neighbors were quite displeased. So they sued to try to shutter the bells.

The neighbors hired legal heavyweight William Rawle to represent their interests and persuade the judge that the bells were a nuisance. The church hired George Washington Biddle to persuade the judge that the bells were a blessing. (The Biddles were, and are, an elite Philadelphia family about whom we'll learn more in the next chapter.)

Rawle invoked Shakespeare in his arguments, comparing the reverend to Macbeth ("Macbeth doth murder sleep"). Biddle retorted that if the rich folk were so bothered, they should follow Horace Greeley's advice and "go West" to get away from the sounds of the bells. Experts for both sides testified about the effect of the bells' ringing on a person's nervous system. For their part, the residents feared their property values were plummeting with each tolling of the bells.

The court sided with the neighbors and summarily silenced the bells. The state supreme court upheld the lower court's decision but allowed the bells to ring for a few minutes a half-hour before Sunday services, with the exception of early-morning services. A year later, the bells were permitted to ring on holidays and for weddings and funerals.

Over the following decades, St. Mark's bells fell completely silent due to wear and disrepair, but they were restored in 1999 and now ring regularly.

There, Washington found refuge at a property owned by Colonel Isaac Franks. The colonel had purchased the home from David Deshler, who had it built in 1752. During the latter half of November 1793, Washington rented the home, where he lived and conducted business with his cabinet members while Philadelphia was plagued with yellow fever. Today, the "Germantown White House" is part of the National Park Service.

By 1799, the Pennsylvania capital left Philadelphia for greener pastures, locating first in Lancaster before settling in Harrisburg, where it remains today. The next year, the national capital followed suit, heading south to D.C.

Chaos, Then Consolidation

DURING THE EARLY TO MID-1800s, Philadelphians seemed to forget that the city had been founded on the idea of brotherly love. By 1810, New York took the lead over Philadelphia as the most populated city. Philadelphia did see a population increase, but most of its newest citizens were poor immigrants from Ireland. These new immigrants were largely Catholic, and great tensions started to rise between them and the Protestant natives. As the city's industrial business grew, lawlessness, rioting, and bloodshed ensued in the streets of Philadelphia proper, which was only about 2 square miles at this point in history. And there was even more trouble happening on the outskirts of the city, in areas such as Kensington and Southwark. There was no way for the city to control people who weren't citizens of Philadelphia. Much of the policing going on in those "suburbs" was happening in the form of town watchmen who had little to no actual police power.

Enter the Consolidation Act of 1854. On February 2, 1854, Philadelphia went from 2 square miles to 129 square miles, pretty much mirroring the boundaries of today's Philadelphia. The population rose from 125,000 to more than half a million citizens overnight. *Boom.* Just like that.

Pennsylvania Governor William Bigler signed the law after much political wrangling. Integral in getting the Consolidation Act passed was Eli Kirk Price, a real estate lawyer who had been previously elected to the Pennsylvania Senate. Kirk was a member of the American Philosophical Society and later became a commissioner to Fairmount

Park. Another prominent Philadelphian and key player in getting the Consolidation Act passed was Morton McMichael. McMichael was the chair of the Executive Consolidation Committee, which was a group of rich Philadelphians who met to put together a draft version of what they would like the consolidation bill to look like. McMichael was a prominent newspaper publisher and later became a mayor.

The Consolidation Act did a number of things for Philadelphia. First and foremost, it made the city competitive again in size. In one fell swoop, the city became the second largest in population in the country. The city enveloped a grand total of 29 municipalities, including Philadelphia proper. And the new city would get a new city hall, to be built at Broad and Market Streets, where it still stands to this day, with William Penn perched high atop the building. Most importantly, though, the act gave the city widespread authority to police the entire boundary of the new Philadelphia. The first mayor under the new city was Robert Conrad, and he would head the new police department created to instill law and order. Conrad hired 900 police officers but refused to hire any immigrants for the new police force. The police department was run from City Hall for decades, before the Department of Public Safety was created and the Director of Public Safety was put in charge of the police department. But despite consolidation, each section of the city held on to its own identity, and even today, Philadelphia is a city of neighborhoods, each with distinct personalities and citizenry.

It was also during this time that the prison system in Philadelphia underwent a major overhaul. Prisoners before the Revolutionary War were often subject to brutality and starvation. One Quaker, Richard Wistar, took it upon himself to have soup made and delivered to the prisons throughout the city to help alleviate starvation. He even formed an advocacy group to take on the cause of prisoners—the Philadelphia Society for Assisting Distressed Prisoners. But after the British soldiers came to the city, the organization shut down. Fast-forward to after the end of the war when another group of prominent citizens, including Benjamin Franklin and Benjamin Rush, again

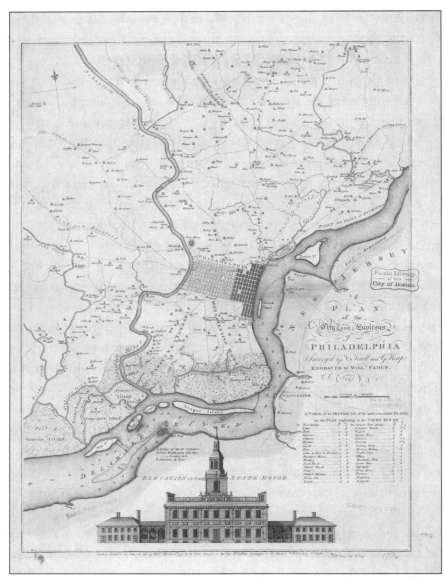

Philadelphia before consolidation in 1854

(Engraving by Will Faden; via Wikimedia Commons, public domain)

advocated for humane treatment of prisoners. In 1787, this group met at Franklin's home to discuss prison reform. This time period was during the Age of Enlightenment, and the institution of democracy

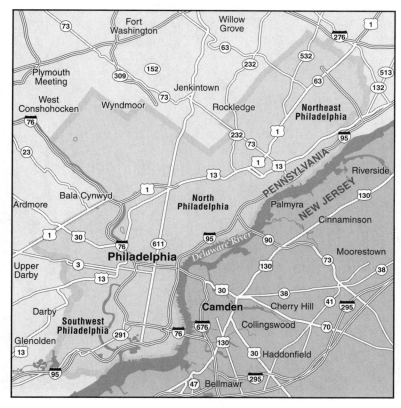

Today's Philadelphia looks much as it did right after consolidation.

(Map by Steve Jones)

was only one of the many changes. The group called themselves The Philadelphia Society for Alleviating the Miseries of Public Prisons. Rush came up with the idea of creating a space for prisoners to be held in solitary confinement so that they may truly repent upon the error of their ways. The term *penitentiary* was born, and the society lobbied the Commonwealth hard to build a new prison to reflect this new "Pennsylvania System." The state finally agreed with the group and agreed to foot the bill to build Eastern State Penitentiary.

Eastern State Penitentiary—originally called Cherry Hill, due to the prison's displacement of a cherry orchard—was built on farmland outside of the city (since it hadn't been consolidated yet). Architect John

Eastern State Penitentiary was a model prison in its day.

(Photo: © M. Fischetti/Visit Philadelphia)

Haviland was hired to build the sprawling structure, which became a marvel of construction. Prisoners had their own private cells and yard, in addition to an area where they could work. Each cell even had central heat, running water, and flush toilets (even before the White House had such amenities!). Tourists came in droves to see the new facility, as did representatives from around the world seeking to copy the Pennsylvania System. The policy of solitary confinement would remain an accepted practice until 1913, but Eastern State stayed open until 1971, when it became too costly to maintain. Today, the prison is still standing and is run by a nonprofit agency that hosts tours and a popular Halloween program. Franklin's prison task force morphed into the Pennsylvania Prison Society, which continues to advocate for the humane treatment of prisoners.

The Philadelphia Lawyer

It's safe to say that Philadelphia is a lawyer's town. Always has been, always will be. Currently, more than 13,000 lawyers practice in the Philadelphia area. It's impossible to document all of the accomplishments of all the lawyers who helped shape Philadelphia, but there are a number of them who were integral to Philadelphia in its formative years. Philadelphia was also home to the first law library—then called the Law Library Company of the City of Philadelphia, and today known as the Jenkins Law Library. In 1802, 71 lawyers pooled their resources to start the library and purchase books. William Rawle was one of the library's founders and its first librarian, creating the country's first law catalog. Today, the library has hundreds of thousands of volumes.

Philadelphia's first lawyer, figuratively, is the man who helped coin the phrase "Philadelphia lawyer." Many consider Andrew Hamilton to be the founder of the Philadelphia legal establishment. According to **dictionary. com,** a Philadelphia lawyer is "a lawyer of outstanding ability at exploiting legal fine points and technicalities." The phrase was originally one of honor, but it has since taken on a somewhat negative connotation. The case that brought the phrase into existence actually took place in New York. In 1735, Hamilton defended a publisher named John

Andrew Hamilton, the original "Philadelphia lawyer"

(Drawing by Jacques Reich; via Wikimedia Commons, public domain)

America's First Kidnapping for Ransom

A LITTLE BOY NAMED CHARLEY ROSS cast an enormous shadow on Philadelphia and the nation in 1874. The city was preparing for its grand Centennial Exhibition of 1876 and was eager to showcase itself as a world-class metropolis.

Charley Ross, 4, and his brother, Walter, 6, were kidnapped from their front yard in Germantown in July of that year. For reasons unknown, the kidnappers released Walter but not Charley.

In her book *We Is Got Him: The Kidnapping that Changed America,* author Carrie Hagen details the saga of the search for little Charley. The kidnappers sent nearly two dozen letters demanding that Christian Ross, the boy's dad, pay $20,000 for his son's safe return.

Philadelphia and the nation went into a panic because they had never dealt with a kidnapping for ransom. The citywide manhunt turned into a nationwide search.

By December, the two men who had been the main suspects in the case were dead of gunshot wounds. One suspect confessed on his deathbed that he had kidnapped the Ross boy, but the suspect died before he could give any further information.

Another man, William Westervelt, was also suspected of being involved in the kidnapping. A jury believed that he was involved and sent him to Eastern State Penitentiary for seven years to think about his wrongdoing in solitary confinement. He maintained his innocence throughout his entire sentence.

Charley Ross was never found, and his final whereabouts remain a mystery. The Charley Project, an online missing-persons database, is named in his memory.

Peter Zenger who was facing charges of seditious libel brought by royal governor William Cosby. Hamilton was allegedly secretly brought from Philadelphia to represent Zenger. In what became known as the first victory for freedom of the press, Hamilton successfully defended Zenger, and people began saying that in order to win a case, one needed to bring in a Philadelphia lawyer. Hamilton, who was in his 80s during the Zenger case, was also well known as a Pennsylvania attorney general.

Two other prominent attorneys in Philadelphia at this time who also served in the post of attorney general were Tench Francis and Benjamin Chew. Although Francis originally came to the colonies to work for Lord Baltimore, he moved to Philadelphia in 1738. He was also a founding trustee of the college that eventually became the University of Pennsylvania. Chew was more well known than Tench and served as the Penn family attorney. In addition to serving as attorney general, Chew was also appointed as register-general and as chief justice of Pennsylvania. Chew was buddies with George Washington and John Adams, and during the time before the war, he was a supporter of the colonies. Chew, however, did not support the Declaration of Independence and was eventually arrested for treason and sent to New Jersey for punishment. Then his mansion in Germantown, known as Cliveden, was overtaken by British soldiers during the Battle of Germantown. Cliveden sustained damage and still shows the scars of war on its

Benjamin Chew served in a variety of legal roles, including chief justice of Pennsylvania.

(Lithograph by C. S. Bradford; via Wikimedia Commons, public domain)

facade. Chew ultimately returned to Pennsylvania in 1778 and served as an appellate-court judge near the end of his life. Each October, reenactors descend on the city streets surrounding Chew's former country home to pretend battle. The British win every year.

One man who became an icon of Philadelphia law was William Rawle. He was friends with Franklin, Rush, and Thomas Paine and was a lover of the US Constitution. Rawle was wildly successful as a lawyer and served as the first US Attorney for the District of Pennsylvania as a Washington appointee. In fact, his private practice was so successful that he turned down two other appointments—one as a federal judge and one as US Attorney General. He also founded the Rawle Law Offices on September 15, 1783, which today is Rawle & Henderson LLP, the oldest law firm in the United States. He loved America and was impassioned about preserving history and fighting for the rights of minorities. He supported equal rights for Native Americans and African Americans and was president of the Pennsylvania Abolition Society. He also founded the Pennsylvania Historical Society and became its first president. For more than 200 years, there was a Rawle in the legal profession in Philadelphia.

John G. Johnson was another giant of the Philadelphia legal world. He wasn't part of the "Old Philadelphia" gang, but he made a name for himself nonetheless. He turned down two offers to become a justice on the US Supreme Court and one offer to be US Attorney General. He was no stranger to the supreme courts, arguing 168 at the federal level and thousands at the state supreme-court level. He was the go-to lawyer for big business during the Industrial Revolution, representing Peter A. B. Widener, William Elkins, John Wanamaker, J. P. Morgan, and other heavy hitters to be discussed in the next chapter. He also defended huge companies in antitrust litigation, including the American Tobacco Company, Standard Oil, and several railroad companies. According to his obituary in *The New York Times,* many judges considered Johnson to be the "greatest lawyer in the English-speaking world." He also was an avid art collector, amassing hundreds of paintings that are now showcased at the Philadelphia Museum of Art.

Another "outsider" to the legal world dominated by Old Philadelphians, Owen J. Roberts became a legal rock star based on his

Leading Ladies: Betsy Ross

EVERYONE KNOWS THAT BETSY ROSS made the first American flag. We all learned that in elementary school, right? Right—except it doesn't seem to be true. She was indeed a flagmaker, but most scholars now believe that she was not the person who made the first American flag.

Betsy Ross was born Elizabeth Griscom in Philadelphia in 1752. She was unlucky in her marriages, with her first two husbands meeting untimely deaths. She married one more time, ultimately becoming Elizabeth Griscom Ross Ashburn Claypoole.

Commonly known as Betsy Ross, she was an upholsterer and seamstress by trade. Legend has it that in 1776 she showed George Washington, Robert Mor-

Betsy Ross: maker of the first American flag?

(Painting by G. Liebscher; via Wikimedia Commons, public domain)

ris, and her uncle-in-law George Ross some fancy fabric star–snipping skills and, in turn, was asked to make the new nation's flag.

However, the story of how the first flag making went down wasn't even told until 1870, when her grandson told it. The story then made it to *Harper's Monthly* a few years later and has since become legend.

The Betsy Ross House is a popular tourist destination, even though there is some debate as to whether she actually lived there.

The story will no doubt live on, regardless of its integrity. But was Betsy Ross the person to make the first American flag? Probably not.

Philadelphia lawyer John G. Johnson amassed a huge collection of artwork.

(Unknown photographer; via Wikimedia Commons, public domain)

involvement at the federal level. Born in Philadelphia in 1875, Roberts graduated from the University of Pennsylvania Law School (Penn Law) in 1907. Within 11 years of graduating from Penn Law, he was appointed Special Assistant US Attorney and was charged with investigating spy cases. He did such an outstanding job that his legal talents were tapped again when he was appointed special counsel in a national political scandal of the 1920s. Before there was Watergate, there was Teapot Dome, which involved shady dealings surrounding oil leases; Roberts's work on the case gave him a reputation that would ultimately land him a seat on the US Supreme Court. Today a school district bears his name near the home and farm he retired to in Chester County. He also founded a law firm now known as Montgomery McCracken Walker & Rhoads LLP.

Because Philadelphia has always been a lawyer's town, it boasts an incredible amount of notable attorneys who contributed to the growth of the city. Here's a short list of notables and what they did.

- **James Wilson** was a signer of the Declaration of Independence, integral in shaping the US Constitution, and one of the original six justices of the US Supreme Court. Wilson is credited with giving the first law lectures at the College of Philadelphia, now the University of Pennsylvania (Penn).

- **George Sharswood** is credited with formally establishing Penn Law in the 1850s. **William Draper Lewis** was the school's first official full-time dean, serving from 1896 to 1914. Lewis also founded the American Law Institute, an independent organization that produces restatements of laws that "work to clarify, modernize, and otherwise improve the law."

- **Jared Ingersoll Jr.** was a Philadelphia lawyer who served in the Continental Congress and was later a delegate to the Constitutional Convention. He was appointed attorney general of Pennsylvania in 1811, and generations of Ingersolls have become members of the Philadelphia bar.

- **George Wharton Pepper** was a well-known constitutional lawyer in the early 20th century. He taught law at Penn Law for more than two decades and served as both the president of the American Law Institute and Chancellor of the Philadelphia Bar Association. He started the law firm today known as Pepper Hamilton LLP.

- **Richard Rush** was the son of the noted Dr. Benjamin Rush (see Chapter 3). He served as both a Pennsylvania and US Attorney General. He was also Secretary of the Treasury and the running mate of John Quincy Adams in his failed run for president. In addition, Rush was integral in facilitating the creation of the Smithsonian Institution from the estate of James Smithson.

- **Horace Binney,** a stately Old Philadelphian, graduated from Harvard Law School. He is most famous for his successful defense of the City of Philadelphia in the case *Vidal v. Philadelphia* against his opposing counsel, the famous Daniel Webster. Stephen Girard left his estate to the City of Philadelphia for the purpose of creating a school for poor, orphaned Philadelphians. Girard's family was displeased with his will and brought the case to court. The case established the legal parameters for the creation of charitable trusts in the United States. Binney's co-counsel was John Sergeant, a notable lawyer in his own right.

William Lewis was a lawyer and later a federal court judge. He was integral in the drafting of the "Act for the Gradual Abolition of Slavery," which was the first legal move designed to end slavery. His home is today called Historic Strawberry Mansion, which is open to the public for tours.

The city's legal community remains as vibrant as ever, and the Old Philadelphia surnames still show themselves regularly in the courtrooms and law offices across the city. And of course, throngs of tourists flock daily to visit Philadelphia to see where the law of our land, the US Constitution, was born.

PHILLY FACT Did you know that Philadelphia police coined the phrase "Black Friday"? In the 1950s and 1960s, they started using the term to refer to the day after Thanksgiving—then as now, a traffic and crowd headache for law enforcement and shoppers everywhere—thinking it would discourage people from coming out. No such luck: Philadelphians came to think the phrase meant the start of the period when stores would go into the black, or turn a profit, and they continued to turn out in droves.

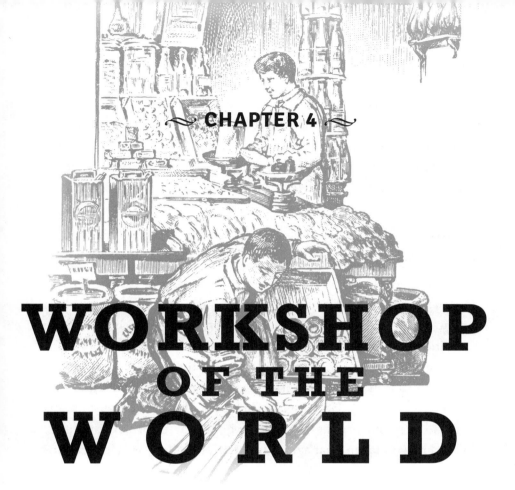

CHAPTER 4

WORKSHOP
OF THE
WORLD

MAGINE THE INTRICACIES that go into weaving a tapestry. You've got the rows and rows of fiber and then the delicate back-and-forth dance with the shuttle to form a pattern. Foot pedal, lift and lower. Hand shuttle, back and forth. Weave. In the end, you have a tightly knit, beautiful work of art.

Now think about Philadelphia during the dawn of the Industrial Revolution and imagine the tight-knit, interwoven industrial society that developed. Philadelphia was a bastion of business because so many people brought their love of innovation to the city and set up shop. The banking system was born and flourished in the fledgling city. And with an easy flow of money, industry started to boom. Philadelphia became known as the "Workshop of the World," because anything and everything was made in Penn's city. Philadelphia defined the idea of a "local economy" eons before it became a trendy buzz phrase. Businesses often sourced their needed materials from other Philadelphia businesses. The boom of industry was further fueled by the development of transportation technology. Railroads, ships, and the creation of mass transit contributed to the growth of business and industry. Throughout it all, several powerful people and families led the way.

Money Changes Everything

THE WORLD OF BANKING came to Philadelphia in 1782, when the first commercial bank opened its doors. The Bank of North America loaned money to both the state and federal governments as well as private businesses across the city. Financier Robert Morris, whom the Continental Congress had previously appointed as its Superintendent of Finance, got the OK from the congress to open his commercial bank, the first in the nation. Morris was born in England and came to America in 1744. He struggled in school, but not because it was hard; to the contrary, he couldn't be bound by a formal education. Instead he was taken in at age 16 by Charles Willing as an apprentice in the counting room of Willing & Co., a mercantile business. After Willing's death two years later, his son Thomas would continue his father's company and partnership with Morris, changing the company's name to Willing Morris & Co. Willing and Morris became financial leaders during the American Revolution and afterward, Willing becoming the first president of the Bank of North America.

After the end of the American Revolution, the country was broke and in debt. Alexander Hamilton came up with the idea to create a central national bank that could both deal with the war debt and standardize a universal form of currency for the country. Up to that point, each state had its own form of money. The first US Mint was approved and became the first federal building constructed under the new Constitution, and it still operates in Philadelphia to this day. The idea of a national bank, however, was controversial because many feared government control of currency. But the bill passed Congress and George Washington signed it, creating the First Bank of the United

Stephen Girard operated the first private bank in the country.

(Drawing by Elbert Hubbard; via Wikimedia Commons, public domain)

States. It was located on Third Street between Chestnut and Walnut Streets, in what is today's Old City section. Thomas Willing would emerge a leader again and take the helm as president of the national bank. The bank operated until 1811 when Congress voted to close it. Enter Stephen Girard.

Girard had a true rags-to-riches story. Born in France, he found his way to America because he was a trader. He landed in Philadelphia in 1776 and continued his self-made trading business. During the American Revolution, when he was unable to trade internationally, he took to merchandising locally. He was quite successful and managed to amass some wealth, which he then invested in real estate and banking. By the time the First Bank of the United States was shuttered, Girard was able to buy the bank's building and all of its accounts. His Bank of Stephen Girard was the first private bank in the country, with a starting capital of $1.2 million. While that amount of money is a lot to us today, it was an insanely large sum in 1810. Girard's bank was so successful that he, along with other wealthy men like John Jacob Astor, was able to help foot the bill for the War of 1812. After that war, the country would again establish a national bank, the Second National Bank of the United States. Girard was a leading supporter of the national bank and showed that support by subscribing to $3 million of stock. Girard kept up his private bank business at the same time and would spend his spare time at his farm in South Philadelphia. When Girard died in 1831, he left most of his $6 million estate to the City of Philadelphia in a trust

Nicholas Biddle, president of the
Second Bank of the United States

*(Painting by William Inman; via Wikimedia
Commons, public domain)*

fund for the establishment of a school for poor white orphans. After a tumultuous legal battle, Girard College was opened in 1848 and still educates underserved youth.

The Second Bank of the United States, like its predecessor, was very controversial. The president of the bank was Nicholas Biddle, a prominent Philadelphian from a well-known, wealthy family. Biddle was born in Philadelphia in 1786 and was a lawyer, literary scholar, and editor. In 1822, Biddle became president of the Second Bank of the United States and led the bank to prosperity for years, opening 29 branches and controlling a large portion of the country's wealth. But President Andrew Jackson hated the bank and vowed to ruin it. Biddle made the bold move of trying to renew the bank's charter four years before it was up for renewal. The charter moved through Congress with approval, but Jackson called the bank a monopoly and vetoed the bill to renew its charter. Biddle then requested and was granted a state charter for the bank, which then became known as the Bank of the United States of Pennsylvania. Biddle retired from the bank three years later in 1839 and went to live at his estate, Andalusia, today a National Historic Landmark, outside of Philadelphia. He also worked to help establish Girard College. His bank, however, ultimately failed in 1841 and took Biddle's money with it.

Another huge contributor to both the Philadelphia and national banking scenes came from the Drexel family. Francis Martin Drexel was an Austrian portrait painter who found his way to Philadelphia in 1817. Twenty years later, he was rich enough to open his own banking house, called Drexel & Company. He and his wife, Catherine Hookey, had six children and a legacy that stands strong in Philadelphia. His sons Francis Anthony and Anthony Joseph would take over their dad's business upon his death and turn Drexel & Company into an investment-banking firm.

Francis Anthony Drexel worked in the family business and had two wives. He and his first wife, Hannah Langstroth, had two daughters, one of whom, Katharine, became a nun and was declared the second US-born Roman Catholic saint 45 years after her death in 1955.

Anthony Joseph Drexel, however, was the brains behind the management of the company. Drexel & Company developed branches across the country and the world, and in 1871, Anthony Drexel formed a private banking partnership in New York with J. Pierpont Morgan called Drexel, Morgan & Company. Their company essentially helped fund the Industrial Revolution, providing financing for the building of railroads, the development of mining operations, and the creation of factories.

That partnership blossomed into what is known today as JP Morgan. Two years before his death, Drexel took some of his riches and invested them in the future by establishing the Drexel Institute of Art, Science, and Technology. Initially a noncollegiate institution, Drexel Institute began offering bachelor's degrees by 1914. Today, that college, now known as Drexel University, includes a law school and medical school and is well known for its cooperative-education program. The name Drexel is everywhere in Philadelphia, and the legacy that Anthony Joseph Drexel started is sure to endure.

Anthony J. Drexel, banking powerhouse

(Unknown photographer; via Wikimedia Commons, public domain)

Reading Terminal Market

The Reading Terminal Market and Railroad Depot

(Engraving by unknown artist, part of the Cooper Collection of American Railroadiana; via Wikimedia Commons, public domain)

IMAGINE A ONE-STOP SHOP for lunch and all the fixings you need to make dinner, dessert, and coffee to boot: Reading Terminal Market has it all. Thousands of Philadelphians go there every day to eat and shop. You'll often see many of those people wearing "juror" badges, because the merchants offer jurors a small discount for eating at the market while on duty. It's often the highlight of the day for anyone doing his or her civic duty.

Business Boom

WITH THE CITY FLUSH WITH MONEY, businesses flourished. Thousands of different kinds of businesses blossomed and made Philadelphia the "Workshop of the World." From 1880 to 1920, Philadelphia made anything and everything, from trains and toys to umbrellas and

Reading Terminal Market got its name from, you guessed it, the Philadelphia & Reading Railroad. The merchants, however, were there before the railroad roared on the scene. The butchers' market and farmers' market sold their goods on Market Street at 11th Street. When the railroad came along and bought the block, the merchants balked and fought for their right to continue to sell their goods at the railroad's terminal. The Reading Terminal Market opened for business in February 1892.

The market flourished for years and also benefited from the industrial boom going on around the city as well as the increase in public transportation. In 1913, the market featured 250 separate food dealers and 100 farmers selling food. The market even fared well during the Great Depression because, as food became scarce elsewhere in the city, farmers were still able to bring food to the Reading Terminal Market to sell.

The market went through growing pains like the rest of the city when manufacturing jobs left in droves. When the city began revitalization efforts in the 1980s, city leaders decided to build a new convention center right next to the market. The merchants again fought for their right to continue to sell their food and goods, and the city sided with them.

The Pennsylvania Convention Center Authority bought the market in 1990 and gave it a multimillion-dollar makeover. Today, the Reading Terminal Market encompasses more than 75 shops that sell everything from fresh meat and fish to spices to flowers to coffee. By the looks of the bustling crowd every day at lunchtime, the city made a good decision.

upholstery. By 1900, there were 7,000 manufacturers. One of the biggest industries was textiles, with 700 of those 7,000 manufacturers involved in making fabrics, from carpets and ribbons to silk and yarn.

Philadelphia made it all. But all was not well in the City of Brotherly Love. The increase in business created a great divide between the haves and have-nots. There was a huge influx of immigrants to the city, providing for a growing workforce but also rising tensions. Poverty also ballooned, and the ups and downs of the financial industry were felt within manufacturing as well. Nevertheless, Philadelphians persevered through it all, and many prospered.

The following is a breakdown of some of the giants of business and industry in Philadelphia before and during the Industrial Age.

- ■ **PAPER** One of the first major industries in Philadelphia opened up in a community known as **RittenhouseTown,** which is today a historic site within Fairmount Park in the city's Germantown section. In 1690, William Rittenhouse and his son Nicholas opened the first paper mill in America along the banks of Monoshone Creek, which at the time was outside the city limits. For 200 years, eight generations of Rittenhouses lived and worked in RittenhouseTown.

- ■ **LOCOMOTIVES** In the late 19th and early 20th centuries, **Baldwin Locomotive Works** was the largest employer in Philadelphia. Started by Matthias W. Baldwin in 1832, the company made steam locomotives that were sold all over the world. The factory was located

435   PHILADELPHIA— BALDWIN LOCOMOTIVE WORKS

Baldwin Locomotive Works was the largest employer in Philadelphia during the city's industrial heyday.

(Unknown photographer; via Wikimedia Commons, public domain)

at Broad and Spring Garden Streets and claimed to be the world's largest maker of locomotives. At the height of its success, it had a workforce 17,000 strong.

■ **MACHINERY** All the factories needed machinery to make their products. Machining moguls Alfred Jenks and William Sellers rose to the challenge. **Alfred Jenks & Son** in Bridesburg was a maker of textile machinery. Sellers, who dabbled in many industrial pursuits, ran **William Sellers & Company,** which manufactured made-to-order machines. He believed that his machines should be designed to meet the needs of specific businesses. His machines were built with integrity and built to last. Also an inventor, Sellers patented numerous machines and served as president of the Franklin Institute from 1864 to 1867. At the institute, he presented a paper about a new system of screws and nuts. This paper had a huge impact on machine technology, and his system became the industry standard. He also worked in the iron and steel industries. His **Edge Moor Iron Company** provided much of the iron for buildings erected for the Centennial Exhibition (see page 68) and provided all of the ironwork (except the cables) for the Brooklyn Bridge.

■ **SAWS** If it had a blade, it probably came from Henry Disston's **Keystone Saw Works.** Founded in 1850, the company, which later changed its name to **Henry Disston & Sons** and became the largest sawmaker in the world, employed 2,500 employees and spanned 64 acres in the city's Tacony section at the height of production.

■ **COWBOY HATS** Yes, the **Stetson** hat was first mass-produced in Philadelphia. In 1865, John B. Stetson set up shop in the city and became the world's largest hatmaker. His biggest seller, based on a hat he had designed as an adventurer in the West, was a broad-brimmed model for cowboys that he called "Boss of the Plains." By 1915, his company employed more than 5,000 workers.

■ **RETAIL** As the economy did well, Philadelphians wanted to buy things. Retailer John Wanamaker met the demand. Wanamaker started a men's clothing business with his brother-in-law, Nathan Brown, called Oak Hall. The business was super-profitable, and Wanamaker took his profits and opened a second location, now named **John Wanamaker & Company,** at Eighth and Chestnut Streets in 1869. Seven years later, he opened the "Grand Depot" to coincide with the city's Centennial Exhibition. The store was huge and set up shop at the Pennsylvania Railroad Depot at 13th and Chestnut Streets. After the world's fair,

John Wanamaker, retail king

(Photo: George Grantham Bain Collection, Library of Congress; via Wikimedia Commons, public domain)

Wanamaker tried to get other merchants to join him within the space, to no avail. So Wanamaker decided to open a new kind of store—a one-stop shop that would become the modern-day department store and ultimately one of the largest retailers in the country.

Another Philadelphia retail icon, **Strawbridge & Clothier,** opened its doors not too far away from Wanamaker's. Justus C. Strawbridge opened a dry-goods shop at Eighth and Market Streets in 1861. He developed a friendship and later a partnership with Isaac H. Clothier. They opened their flagship store in 1868 and remained in business for 168 years. They also opened a discount chain known as Clover.

Historic rivals, Wanamaker's and Strawbridge's were sold to the May Company in 1995 and 1996, respectively. The former locations of both stores operated as Strawbridge's before being sold to Macy's in 2006.

■ **STEEL** While most of his business was located outside of Philadelphia, Joseph Wharton was still a native son and a steel mogul. In 1857 he was one of the founders of the Saucon Iron Company, which would ultimately become **Bethlehem Steel.** He was also well known for being the first to produce a pure malleable nickel. A mover and shaker, Wharton was also involved in the railroad and coal industries. A founder of Swarthmore College, he also gave the University of Pennsylvania a large donation to establish a business school. The **Wharton School of Finance and Commerce** was the first college-level business school in the country.

■ **SUGAR** Since Philadelphia isn't in a tropical location, it's somewhat surprising that sugar refining was big business here once upon a time. But if we remember that Philadelphia was once the second largest city in the US, and that people love their sweets, it makes sense. In 1900,

117 candy and chocolate makers dotted the Philadelphia landscape. And there were 1,000 candy shops. One of the biggest sugar refineries was **Franklin Sugar Refinery.** The **Pennsylvania Sugar Refining Company** was located in the city's Fishtown section and, in its heyday, encompassed 18 buildings. One of its last remnants came tumbling down, literally, when it was imploded in 1997. The Sugar House Casino is now located there.

- **SHIPBUILDING** Philadelphia is not located on an ocean, yet it became a shipbuilding capital during the Industrial Age. The biggest shipbuilder, **William Cramp & Sons,** was located on the Delaware River, taking up 52 acres of shoreline in the city's Kensington section. Cramp's company built merchant, leisure, and fighting ships for the United States in addition to selling vessels internationally.

- **TEXTILES** Unlike its metal-manufacturing colleagues, Philadelphia's textile industry, although incredibly successful, did not seem to produce superstars. In 1850, the city's textile factories had a production value of more than $64 million. The leading textile was wool, with 20 percent of the country's wool making its way into Philadelphia mills and factories. In 1857, Philly had more textile factories than any other city in the world. Of all the kinds of textiles it produced, Philadelphia was well known for its carpets. Two of the biggest carpetmakers were **John Bromley & Sons,** the oldest such business in the city, and the **James Dobson Carpet Mills** at the Falls of Schuylkill.

- **PHARMACEUTICALS** A global pharmaceutical giant has its roots in Philadelphia. Philadelphian John K. Smith opened a small drugstore on North Second Street in 1830 and then went on to create John K. Smith & Company, a drug-wholesaling company. The company underwent several changes and became Smith, Kline & Company in 1875. Fast-forward several decades and iterations of the company, and after a merger with a European competitor, **GlaxoSmithKline** emerged in 2000.

All of this growth and prosperity in Philadelphia during the Industrial Age were made possible because of the increasing mobility Philadelphians gained due to expanding transportation technology. Philadelphians were going places, literally and figuratively.

The Centennial Celebration

An overview of the grounds for the Centennial International Exhibition of 1876

(Engraving by unknown artist; via Wikimedia Commons, public domain)

IN 1876, Philadelphia held a big bash. It was called The International Exhibition of Arts, Manufactures and Products of the Soil and Mine, or simply the Centennial Exhibition. It was a party that lasted for six

Going Places

ALL OF THOSE FACTORIES needed fuel to run all of those machines. One of the things that helped Philadelphia become a manufacturing powerhouse was the city's proximity to coal. Coal was king through-out the Keystone State, and Philadelphians needed to find a way to months, and all the coolest Americans attended. It was essentially the first world's fair.

Planning for the centennial was not slight by any means. The city built 200 buildings, costing Philadelphia $10 million. A special railroad depot was built, and a special train took people to the different exhibits. The city dug lakes, built monuments and statues, and planted 20,000 trees and shrubs. Ain't no party like a Philly party.

The idea was to celebrate 100 years of freedom, but the themes of the centennial were more focused on science and innovation than on patriotism and national pride. Throughout the six months of the Centennial Exhibition, 10 million visitors came to the City of Brotherly Love. Opening day alone saw 200,000 people.

Tons of inventions were on display, including something called the telephone, created by a guy named Alexander Graham Bell, and the phonograph, created by a young chap named Thomas Edison.

Dignitaries from around the world visited Philadelphia during the centennial, which drew positive reviews from around the globe. Philadelphia showed the rest of the country and the world what it meant to be an American.

Many of the buildings erected for the Centennial Exhibition still stand tall in Philadelphia, including Memorial Hall, which now houses the Please Touch Museum, where wee ones are encouraged to interact completely with the exhibitions.

get it easily. New York City had been competing with Philadelphia for years and had taken the lead after the building of the Erie Canal. Philadelphians were late to the canal race but managed to make a showing. The Schuylkill Canal was opened for business in 1825 and connected Philadelphia to Port Carbon, which was just north of Reading. Philadelphia had already been getting coal for a few years, but the completion of the canal enabled the city to obtain more. However, the usefulness of the canal would soon fall victim to the railroad industry.

Philadelphia was in major competition with New York and Baltimore to remain the control center of the nation's commerce. With New York getting the Erie Canal and Baltimore getting the Baltimore and Ohio Railroad, the pressure was really on. The Pennsylvania Railroad (PRR) was born in 1846. When construction was complete, the PRR ran across the state from Pittsburgh to Philadelphia. It continued to expand outside the Keystone State to Baltimore, Washington, New York, and even westward to Chicago. By 1910, the PRR was the leading railroad system in the country. That year it employed 215,000 people, had routes crisscrossing 13 states, and boasted more than a quarter-million freight and passenger cars.

Many Philadelphia leaders were involved in the PRR. An early supporter was Samuel Vaughan Merrick, whom we read about in Chapter 2 due to his involvement in founding The Franklin Institute. Merrick was a manufacturer of heavy machinery, boilers, and engines. He was also the chief engineer for the city as it figured out how to pipe gas to light Philadelphia streets. One year after the PRR opened its doors for business, Merrick became the company's first president. He led the company through its early years and remained its leader until he felt it was certain to be a success. He resigned in 1849 but remained involved for three more years.

Another rail company that started operation before the PRR never had the same success, but the Philadelphia & Reading Railroad (P&R) did transport much-needed coal to the city's factories. The P&R started in 1842 and ran along the Schuylkill River, creating direct competition for the Schuylkill River Canal. In 1870, Philadelphia native Franklin B. Gowen took over as president of the P&R and led it to great success. A lawyer by trade, Gowen had previously served as the district attorney for Schuylkill County, where he successfully prosecuted the case of the Molly Maguires. His plan for the P&R was to buy coal lands for the railroad to expand its ability to transport black gold. He would later open up Port Richmond (a riverfront neighborhood in today's Philadelphia) so

Leading Ladies: Suffragists

Lucretia Mott fought for equal rights for African Americans and women.

(Unknown photographer; via Wikimedia Commons, public domain)

SEVERAL PROMINENT PHILADELPHIA WOMEN were integral to the women's rights movement in the US.

Lucretia Coffin Mott fought for the rights of both African Americans and women. She was born in Massachusetts in 1793. She married a fellow Quaker, James Mott, and the two made Philadelphia their home in 1811.

Considered a radical for her time, Mott often faced threats due to her support of the abolition of slavery. In 1840, Mott and her husband went to the World's Anti-Slavery Convention in London where she and other women in attendance were not allowed to fully participate. When she came back to the United States, she and Elizabeth Cady Stanton joined forces to organize the Seneca Falls Convention in 1848. She would fight for women's rights for the rest of her life. In 1864, she helped to found Swarthmore College, just outside of Philadelphia. She died in 1880 and is buried at Fairhill Burial Ground, the final resting place for numerous famous Philadelphia Quakers and civil rights leaders.

Two other women active in the suffrage movement in Philadelphia were **Dora Lewis** and **Caroline Katzenstein.** Katzenstein came to Philadelphia in 1907 and quickly joined the suffrage movement. In 1910, she became the secretary when the Pennsylvania Woman Suffrage Association and the Women Suffrage Society joined to open their headquarters in Philadelphia. She helped found the National Woman's Party, which worked hard to try to pass an Equal Rights Amendment to the Constitution. Lewis was from a prominent Philadelphia family and was an officer in the National Woman's Party.

that coal could be loaded onto ships and exported. His leadership of the P&R netted the company profits in the hundreds of millions of dollars.

The addition of commuter rail lines also allowed Philadelphians, particularly those in the middle class, to move farther away from their place of work. The first commuter line, the Philadelphia, Germantown, & Norristown Railroad, opened in 1832. After the city's consolidation in 1854, horse-drawn streetcars became the preferred method of transportation. But the 1890s saw the dawn of the subway and elevated train. Philadelphia business moguls P. A. B. Widener and William Lukens Elkins would become the kings of the traction train movement in Philadelphia and elsewhere. Elkins had made money in a number of business ventures. He built the first large refrigerator in the city, capable of holding large amounts of produce. He was also involved in the oil business and was a partner in Standard Oil Company. Widener started growing his fortune with mutton. During the Civil War, he got a huge contract from the US government to give mutton to all the soldiers in the Philadelphia area. He sold $50,000 worth of mutton. He was an investor in steel, tobacco, oil, and railroads. In 1875, Widener and Elkins created the Philadelphia Traction Company, which eventually morphed into the Philadelphia Rapid Transit Company (PRTC). The PRTC opened the Market–Frankford Line in 1907 and the Broad Street Subway in sections from 1928 to 1932. The company reorganized and was eventually bought out by the Southeastern Pennsylvania Transportation Authority, or SEPTA, in 1965.

> **PHILLY FACT** During the industrial boom, Philadelphia was well known for making everything under the sun, including porcelain false teeth. **S. S. White Dental Works** employed hundreds of people and churned out millions of dentures and other dental supplies.

The PRR survived the Great Depression, but when manufacturing started leaving Philadelphia in the 1950s and 1960s and cars became the preferred method of transportation, the company's profits plummeted. The company reorganized but ultimately sold out to Conrail and Amtrak. The P&R suffered a similar fate. And what was a boom for Philadelphia back then eventually became a bust for the city when the Workshop of the World closed shop. Factories closed, jobs disappeared, and the city went into an identity crisis.

The Industrial Age certainly fortified Philadelphia as a city of neighborhoods, many of which had strengthened and taken shape during the manufacturing age. Philadelphia still has the vestiges of a bygone industrial era. Old factories have been converted into hip new housing, and the areas closest to Center City have seen revitalization. Driving around the city, you can certainly feel the vibes from the age of innovation, and those vibes continue to drive Philadelphians to reinvent their city.

~ CHAPTER 5 ~

RAILROAD
TO
FREEDOM

PHILADELPHIA MAY HAVE BEEN FOUNDED as the City of Brotherly Love, but in the beginning there wasn't a whole lot of that love to go around for the African American population who had come to call the city their home. Even before William Penn set foot in Philadelphia, slavery existed. Historians say that both Swedish and Dutch settlers enslaved Africans. And the great men of Philadelphia, including Penn and Benjamin Franklin, owned slaves. Slavery was nowhere near as culturally entrenched here as it was in the South; nevertheless, much of Philadelphia was built on the sweat and blood of African Americans.

But as Philadelphia's population exploded, so did support for the abolition of slavery. As the city became a stronghold for free blacks, however, there was constant tension surrounding the rights of African Americans. As has been the case with other aspects of society, Philadelphia was home to numerous firsts in the struggle for equality in the infant nation, and numerous Philadelphians contributed to the movement for racial equality and freedom.

Penn and Franklin eventually came around to seeing the injustice and inhumanity of slavery, but only after decades of owning slaves themselves. Penn provided for the freedom of his slaves in his will, but because he died poor, his slaves were auctioned off to pay debts. Franklin, on the other hand, owned slaves for about 30 years before becoming an advocate for the abolition of slavery. He even served as a president of Pennsylvania's first abolitionist society.

> **PHILLY FACT** Philadelphia's **African American Museum** opened in 1976 as part of the city's Bicentennial celebration. It was the first museum of its kind in a major city. Its mission is to preserve, interpret, and exhibit the heritage and history of African Americans.

Quakers: Friend or Foe?

MANY QUAKERS, otherwise known as the Religious Society of Friends, contrary to popular belief, trafficked in slavery in the early years of Philadelphia's history. Even Penn's right-hand man, James Logan, was a slave owner. One of his slaves, known as Sampson, was alleged to have run away after burning down a building on his property. Benjamin Chew, the wealthy lawyer and onetime chief justice of the Pennsylvania Supreme Court (see Chapter 3), was another Quaker who trafficked heavily in the slave trade.

Logan and Chew both owned homes in Germantown, which at the time was outside Philadelphia proper. In 1688, Germantown also became home to the first official protest condemning the evils of slavery, signed by four German Quakers, including Daniel Pastorius. Pastorius was a lawyer and a teacher who drafted the protest that said in part, "There is a saying that we shall do to all men like as we will be done ourselves; making no difference of what generation descent or

The Paradox of Freedom

ONE OF THE BIGGEST MARKS on George Washington's legacy is that he owned slaves. In fact, while he was president and living in Philadelphia fighting for freedom, he had nine enslaved African Americans in his household and hundreds more at his home in Virginia.

The President's House was home to Washington and John Adams while Philadelphia was still the capital of the United States. Except for the time he spent in Germantown escaping yellow fever, Washington lived in the President's House from November 1790 to March 1797.

While there, he brought nine of his slaves from his home in Mount Vernon, in direct violation of the Gradual Abolition Law. The law said that enslaved African Americans of non-Pennsylvanian slaveholders could get their freedom after living in Pennsylvania for six months. Washington ignored that part of the law, and he was careful to leave Pennsylvania every six months so that he would not establish any legal residency in the state and have to abide by the law.

The nine enslaved Africans who were forced to live in Philadelphia in Washington's household were Austin, Giles, Hercules, Moll, Oney Judge, Paris, Joe Richardson, Richmond, and Christopher Sheels. Eventually they were replaced with white indentured servants.

color they are. And those who steal or rob men, and those who buy or purchase them, are they not all alike?" Pastorius brought the protest to his local Germantown meeting, but they believed it was too great an issue to take up on the local level, so the protest was pushed along higher and higher through the meeting. Ultimately it went nowhere, but Pastorius's protest began to plant the seeds of doubt among Quakers who thought that slavery was an acceptable practice.

The house, however, and how it is memorialized were the focus of much scrutiny in the new millennium. The mansion had fallen into disrepair over the decades and was demolished to make way for Independence Mall in the 1950s. A public bathroom was erected in 1954 directly on top of where the President's House once stood.

In 2000, when a dig began to build a new site to house the Liberty Bell, excavators unearthed the foundation of the President's House. It also came to light that the entrance of the new Liberty Bell Center would be mere feet away from where Washington housed his slaves. Activists seized this opportunity to tell the truth about Washington and his slaves. Public debate ensued, and pressure mounted for the building of a memorial in recognition of the slaves.

In 2007, the National Park Service commissioned an archaeological dig and constructed a viewing area so people could watch. More than 300,000 curious visitors stopped by to view the dig.

In 2010, a new memorial exhibit called "President's House: Freedom and Slavery in the Making of a New Nation" made its debut. This open-air exhibit features an outline of the original buildings and some of the original foundations. The exhibit also details the history, biography, and roles of all nine of Washington's slaves.

The site is open to visitors 24-7, is steps away from the Liberty Bell, and is a constant reminder of the paradox of freedom during the nation's formative years.

On April 14, 1775, Anthony Benezet and nine other Quakers formed the Society for the Relief of Free Negroes Unlawfully Held in Bondage, the first organization in Philadelphia and the colonies at large dedicated solely to the abolition of slavery. Nine years later, the name would change to the Pennsylvania Society for Promoting the Abolition of Slavery and the Relief of Free Negroes Unlawfully Held in Bondage. It was commonly called the Pennsylvania Abolition

Society and was the very same organization that Franklin became a president of after he changed his stance on slavery.

Benezet immigrated to the US when he was 17 with his family, Protestant Huguenots who had fled religious persecution in France and who came to Philadelphia to be part of Penn's Holy Experiment. In addition to serving as president of the Pennsylvania Abolition Society, Benezet took up teaching at the Friends' English School (now William Penn Charter School). In 1750, he began teaching the children of slaves in his home after regular school hours. He also was integral in starting the first secondary girls' school in the country and created the Negro School for the education of black children. Benezet died in 1784, and Ben Franklin began leading the organization three years later. Today Benezet is recognized as the father and founder of the abolitionist movement in America.

Despite Benezet's efforts, many Quakers hesitated to free their slaves, even though there was growing pressure from the Society of Friends. It took nearly 100 years for the Quakers to issue an ultimatum to their congregants. In 1758, the Philadelphia Yearly Meeting began officially condemning slavery and decided to remove any slaveholders from positions of leadership in the group. Social pressure continued to mount among Quakers, who encouraged fellow Friends to either free their slaves or get the boot from the faith. By 1776, most Quakers chose their faith and freed those bound in servitude to them.

Another first came out of Philadelphia a few years later on the coattails of the American Revolution. In 1780, Pennsylvania passed the country's first abolition law, but it brought freedom only gradually. The Act for the Gradual Abolition of Slavery prohibited Pennsylvanians from legally importing slaves but did nothing to free current slaves. What the law *did* do was free any child born into slavery after the passage of the act, though not until the child turned 28 years old.

From Slavery to Liberty

PHILADELPHIA EVENTUALLY BECAME a Mecca for free African Americans. During the 1790s, the black population in the city tripled, and within 30 years, more than 10 percent of Philadelphia's population was of African descent. Many reasons accounted for the increase, including the escalation in abolitionist activity and the development of schools and churches for African Americans. Two of the men at the forefront of black society at the time were Richard Allen and Absalom Jones.

Allen was born a slave of the family of wealthy Germantown lawyer Benjamin Chew. Allen, his parents, and his siblings all lived as slaves at Chew's country estate, Cliveden, which later became the site of the Battle of Germantown. Allen was 7 years old when he and his family were sold to a Delaware farmer named Stokeley Sturgis. Ten years later, Sturgis sold Allen's mother and three of his siblings, and Allen would never see those family members again. Allen and his brother remained at the Delaware farm and turned to God. Around the time his family was sold, Allen converted to Methodism. Methodists were adamantly opposed to slavery and spoke of punishment in the afterworld for those who participated in the slave trade. Allen persuaded

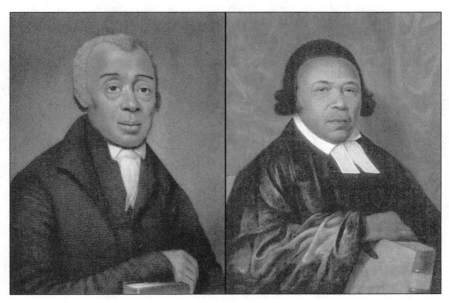

Richard Allen (left) and Absalom Jones founded two of the first African American churches in the US and together founded the Free African Society.

(Painting of Richard Allen by unknown artist; painting of Absalom Jones by Raphaelle Peale; both via Wikimedia Commons, public domain)

A stained-glass window at Mother Bethel AME Church, one of the oldest African American congregations in the US

(Photo: © R. Kennedy/Visit Philadelphia)

Sturgis to allow him to work to buy his freedom. Allen worked as much as he could, and by age 20 he had saved the necessary $2,000. He moved back to Philadelphia and began his odyssey of uniting free and enslaved blacks through religion.

Allen had begun preaching while living in Delaware and had earned a good reputation. Upon his return to Philadelphia, the leadership at

St. George's Methodist Church, a white congregation, invited Allen to preach at its 5 a.m. service. Allen preached throughout the city as well, and African Americans began flocking to St. George's to hear him speak. Around this time, Allen befriended Absalom Jones, a fellow preacher. Jones, too, had been born into slavery and purchased his freedom. As Allen's popularity grew, so did the number of African American parishioners at St. George's, much to the dismay of the white congregants. In an attempt to isolate the black parishioners, St. George's built a balcony at their church. Outside of their work with the church, Allen and Jones united to start the Free African Society, a social-welfare group that acted somewhat like a church in helping unite African Americans in Philadelphia. The FAS helped the sick, homeless, and generally downtrodden.

Meanwhile, tensions continued to flare at St. George's, and the tipping point came in November 1787, when Jones and Allen sat in what they believed to be their new seats in the renovated church. St. George's failed to mention to its African American parishioners that they would need to worship in the new balcony. An elder in the church approached Jones and tried to pull him up from kneeling to bodily remove him to the balcony. Jones peacefully resisted and informed the elder he would move after prayer. When prayers were over, Jones and Allen left St. George's, never to return, along with many black parishioners. After that incident, Allen and Jones set out on their own to establish their own churches.

Allen remained in the Methodist faith and was ordained as the first black Methodist minister in 1799. Allen also worked tirelessly throughout his life for official recognition of the African Methodist Episcopal (AME) Church, the first black Protestant denomination in the world. He became the church's first bishop, and he also helped establish Mother Bethel AME Church, the denomination's first congregation.

Allen was, of course, an abolitionist, and Mother Bethel AME was a stop on the Underground Railroad. Today, the AME church has more than 2.5 million members. Both Allen and Jones continued to work with the Free African Society and The African Church, a congregation that had developed from the FAS. Most of the people in the group preferred the Episcopal faith to the Methodist faith, even though Allen and Jones preferred the latter. So while Allen went off to found Mother Bethel AME, Jones continued to work with The African Church, which became The African Episcopal Church of St. Thomas. In 1802, Jones became the first African American ordained as an Episcopal priest. Both men worked with the sick during the Yellow Fever Epidemic of 1793, which put their church projects on hold. Jones opened his church first on July 17, 1794, making St. Thomas the first black Episcopal congregation in America. Mother Bethel AME held its dedication service on July 29 of the same year.

As more enslaved Africans became free, a movement began among whites to send them back to Africa. The American Colonization Society (ACS) started in 1816 with the intent of repatriating free blacks, specifically to a new African colony called Liberia. While some ACS members were abolitionists who sincerely felt that former slaves would have better lives in Africa, other members were slaveholders who believed that free blacks were incapable of assimilating into white society and posed a threat to civil order by creating unrest among slaves. Although some free African Americans embraced repatriation, most opposed it—they now saw the United States as their home and wanted to become full, equal citizens.

James Forten opposed the American Colonization Society's "back to Africa" campaign.

(Painting by unknown artist; via Wikimedia Commons, public domain)

Enter James Forten. A wealthy, free-born businessman who had established himself as a sailmaker, Forten fought for the rights of all African Americans. Together with Allen and Jones,

Forten held a meeting at Mother Bethel AME that drew approximately 3,000 Philadelphians who were opposed to the ACS and its aims. Their voices were heard, and historians believe this meeting marked a turning point in the fight to push African Americans out of the country. Forten continued to fight for abolition and equality for the rest of his life.

Headed for Freedom

GIVEN ITS PROXIMITY TO THE SOUTH, Philadelphia, and Pennsylvania in general, became the first stop on the Underground Railroad—the name given to the journey to freedom of formerly enslaved African Americans. It is within this part of Philadelphia society where there was boundless love for African Americans and their dream to be free and treated equally. Judge Richard Peters, a white abolitionist, made quite a statement in 1800 when he decided a case involving 134 enslaved Africans being illegally transported via ships. A US Navy ship intercepted the two ships and found that slaves were aboard, in direct violation of the 1794 Slave Trade Law. Peters determined that the Pennsylvania Abolition Society should become responsible for them, and the society in turn freed all of them. Today, Peters's home, Belmont Mansion, is open for tours and is home to the Underground Railroad Museum.

Probably the most prominent African American to help slaves escape bondage was William Still. The youngest of 18 children, Still was born free to enslaved parents. He moved to Philadelphia in 1844 and began working for the Pennsylvania Society for the Abolition of Slavery. He quickly became active in the Underground Railroad. The Fugitive Slave Acts were federal laws that set out to return runaway slaves and punish those who helped them obtain freedom. Still was unfazed by these laws and worked tirelessly to help free his enslaved brethren. He never took notes or kept records of his activities until one day when his brother showed up at his door, having bought his own freedom. Still took this reunion as a sign that he should document everything if it could help other lost loved ones reunite. During the 1850s, he is said to have helped nearly 1,000 former slaves find their freedom. Mostly men, they came to Pennsylvania because it had the largest free African American population—approximately 56,000 before the start of the Civil War.

When the Civil War broke out, Still hid all of his documents in a safe place: a cemetery. When the war was over and slavery was abolished, he gathered all of his papers and wrote a book called *The Underground Railroad: A Record,* which was widely read and even exhibited at Philadelphia's grand Centennial Exhibition of 1876. The book is still in print and is also freely available at the Project Gutenberg website (**gutenberg.org**).

One of the stops on the Underground Railroad through Philadelphia was a Germantown home now known as the Johnson House. John Johnson, a Quaker who was the son of a Dutch immigrant, built the home in 1768. Johnson's son Samuel also made the house his homestead, but he and his wife, Jennet, opened it up to those seeking refuge on their journey toward freedom. The Johnsons gave shelter, food, clothes, and transportation to numerous former slaves. Although undocumented, tradition says that Still and legendary abolitionist Harriet Tubman visited the Johnson House on occasion. Today, the house is a museum and open for tours.

An Uneasy Freedom

WHAT NEWLY FREE BLACKS found in Philadelphia was no racial utopia. To the contrary, many white Philadelphians had only contempt for their new neighbors. Race riots were commonplace, and violence against African Americans was a constant threat. An example of the hatred blacks faced regularly in Philadelphia society was the burning of Pennsylvania Hall. Abolitionists gathered together to build their own meeting space because they had a difficult time renting space in the city. The doors opened in May 1838, only to be surrounded by an angry mob of thousands who set the hall on fire, torched a nearby black orphanage, and attacked a black church.

Throughout these tumultuous times, one figure emerged as an ardent activist for African Americans in the city and the country at large. Octavius Catto was born free in South Carolina and came to Philadelphia sometime in the mid-1800s. He attended school in Philadelphia and studied at the first black college in the region, now known as Cheyney University. Catto supported the Union during the Civil War and served in the Pennsylvania National Guard as a major and inspector. While training near Philadelphia, Catto became interested in baseball, and he ultimately helped form an all-black team, the Pythian Base Ball Club.

Catto was extremely vocal in the battle to desegregate Philadelphia's trolley cars during the 1860s. On May 18, 1865, he committed an act of civil disobedience that Rosa Parks would echo nearly a century later. Catto was on a trolley and refused to get off when told to do so. In response, the conductor purposely derailed the car and left Catto there by himself. Catto stayed there all night, and people gathered to see his act of peaceful protest. The story even made the national news. Catto continued to fight for desegregation and helped get a desegregation law passed in March 1867.

And the tide was ever so slowly turning in the United States. In 1870, the 15th Amendment

Octavius Catto fought to desegregate Philadelphia's trolleys.

(Unknown photographer; via Wikimedia Commons, public domain)

Henry "Box" Brown

Henry "Box" Brown mailed himself to freedom in Philadelphia.

(Engraving from The Underground Railroad: A Record, *by William Still; via Wikimedia Commons, public domain)*

WHILE NOT A CERTIFIED PHILADELPHIAN, Henry "Box" Brown's story is so inspirational that no narrative of African American history in Philadelphia would be complete without it.

Brown was born enslaved in Virginia in 1815. He was a domestic slave for most of his youth, but after his master died, his new master forced him to work in a tobacco factory. His new master, however, often rewarded Brown with small sums of money for his work.

Brown later requested permission to marry a house slave named Nancy. They married, got their own home, and had several children. Unfortunately, after 12 years, Nancy and her children were sold and forced to move to an unknown location.

Brown then made it his mission to break free. Along with two accomplices, James Caesar Anthony Smith and Samuel Smith, he devised a plan to mail himself to Philadelphia, where he could be free.

He consulted with a local carpenter who crafted a shipping crate large enough to fit Brown. On March 19, 1849 he sealed himself in the crate, marked THIS SIDE UP, and set off on his 27-hour journey. He had drilled holes in the crate for air and had taken water with him.

When he arrived at the antislavery organization that was expecting him, his Philadelphia connections—including William Still—feared the worst. But when they opened the box, Brown emerged alive and free.

In the terminology of today, his story went viral. His accomplices in Virginia were found out and arrested, but Brown lived the rest of his life free, later moving to Boston.

gave black males the right to vote. The first time African Americans could vote in Philadelphia, a unit of the Marines was on hand to ensure no violence erupted against new voters, but all was quiet.

On October 10, 1871, Catto was eager to cast his second vote in the general election. By that time, the polls had become segregated and blacks had to vote later in the day than whites. Even though Catto and others requested military support to guarantee peace, the military authorities said no. A roving gang of Irish immigrants trolled city streets trying to intimidate blacks into not voting. Catto encountered a group of angry white people and felt threatened. He headed toward the mayor's office to find help. Again, he came across another group of angry men, and this time they pointed a gun at him. He escaped harm and went to buy a gun himself. He was on his way to his home near Eighth and South Streets to get bullets when someone called out to him. The man, Frank Kelly, fired three shots into Catto, killing him instantly. Thousands turned out for his funeral, and his death cast a pall over the city. Kelly fled the city to be found six years later and extradited to Philadelphia to face murder charges. Even though six witnesses identified him as the shooter, the all-white jury found him not guilty.

African Americans in Modern Philadelphia

PHILADELPHIA HAS CLEARLY had its shining moments in the plight of African Americans seeking freedom, as well as its undeniably shameful moments. Regardless, African Americans continued to migrate to Philadelphia, often in search of a better life. For much of the period of the Industrial Revolution, unfortunately, Philadelphia blacks were not invited to work in most factories. Businesses needed workers but feared that hiring African Americans for those jobs would cause tumult at the workplace. There was at least one exception: The Midvale Steel Company, located in the Nicetown section of the city, welcomed black workers and allowed those workers to have management jobs, all without any conflict.

During this time period, African Americans otherwise worked mostly at domestic jobs. It took World War II draining much of the workforce in Philadelphia before blacks were welcomed into industrial jobs. But soon thereafter, Philadelphia started seeing its industrial jobs fleeing the city, just as thousands of blacks had come north during the early years of the Great Migration. It was during the postwar years that the city experienced a major wave of white flight.

The civil rights era in Philadelphia saw the rise of a giant who fought for the rights of African Americans. Cecil B. Moore was born in West Virginia in 1915 and fought in World War II. Afterward, he moved to Philadelphia to attend law school at Temple University on the GI Bill. Moore quickly earned a reputation as a no-nonsense defense lawyer and tireless advocate for African American rights in civil rights cases. He ultimately became president of Philadelphia's chapter of the NAACP and fought for the desegregation of Philadelphia worksites, particularly those with building trade unions. While some think that his aggressive leadership style may have contributed to the Columbia Avenue race riot of August 1964, he is also credited with helping restore calm in the wake of the violence and vandalism that broke out. Moore also led the successful charge to desegregate Girard College, a preparatory school for underprivileged youth (see Chapter 4), in 1968. In his honor, the stretch of Columbia Avenue from Front to 33rd Street was renamed Cecil B. Moore Avenue in 1987.

And despite the large population of African Americans in Philadelphia, the first black mayor didn't take the city's helm until 1984, when W. Wilson Goode won that position. Unfortunately, his legacy would always be besmirched by an incident known as the MOVE bombing. MOVE consisted of a group of back-to-nature African Americans, many of whom adopted the last name Africa. Neighbors complained to police saying that MOVE members protested through bullhorns at all hours of the night and created numerous health hazards. Police attempted to remove members from their house on the 6200 block of Osage Avenue with little success. On May

Cecil B. Moore, civil rights titan

(Photo: Philadelphia Evening Bulletin, *2/16/1967, from the George D. McDowell* Philadelphia Evening Bulletin *Collection; courtesy of Special Collections Research Center, Temple University Libraries)*

13, 1985, police began a siege on the property that ended with dropping an explosive device on the roof of the compound. The device, however, ignited a gasoline storage tank on the roof and caused a massive fire that left 11 people dead and 61 homes incinerated. MOVE left a lasting scar on the city's history.

Since Goode, the city has elected two African American mayors—John F. Street and Michael Nutter. Currently, African Americans make up approximately 44 percent of the city's population and are well represented in city government.

Leading Ladies: Abolitionists

With her mother and sisters, Harriet Forten Purvis helped start the Philadelphia Female Anti-Slavery Society.

(Unknown photographer; via Wikimedia Commons, public domain)

WOMEN WERE VITAL TO THE FIGHT to end slavery. In Philadelphia, the women of the Forten family were leaders in that fight.

James Forten (see page 82) and his wife, **Charlotte Vandine Forten,** had three daughters—**Margaretta, Harriet,** and **Sarah**— all of whom joined the fight to abolish slavery. Charlotte and her daughters helped start the Philadelphia Female Anti-Slavery Society, which was the first racially integrated women's abolition group.

Harriet and Sarah both married into the Purvis family. Harriet and her husband, Robert, hosted numerous abolitionists and fugitive slaves. She raised five of her own children as well as her niece, **Charlotte Forten Grimké,** a teacher, writer, and prominent abolitionist.

Lucretia Mott (see page 71) and **Mary Ann M'Clintock** also helped found the Philadelphia Female Anti-Slavery Society. They were also two of the five delegates to the Seneca Falls Convention for women's suffrage.

Sarah Pugh was another notable abolitionist leader in Philadelphia. She was a teacher who started her own school. In 1838, when an angry pro-slavery group burned Pennsylvania Hall during the first gathering of the Anti-Slavery Convention of American Women, the abolitionists would not be silenced or stopped and continued their convention at Pugh's school. Pugh also helped establish several schools for freed slaves.

~ CHAPTER 6 ~

GREENE COUNTRIE TOWNE

M ILLIONS OF YEARS AGO, before skyscrapers, oil refineries, and highways were built, Philadelphia was verdant. At the end of the last ice age, sea levels rose, causing a rise in rivers and other tributaries as the tides slogged forward. One of those swollen rivers was the Delaware, which begins its flow in the Catskill Mountains in New York and wends its way through Pennsylvania and New Jersey before finally dumping into the Atlantic Ocean between Maryland and Delaware. The Schuylkill River, one of the major tributaries of the mighty Delaware, bookends Philadelphia to the west.

When William Penn arrived at his new land hundreds of years ago, his dream was to create a "greene countrie towne." As discussed in Chapter 1, he envisioned large parcels of land for property owners, with enough space for each lot to have its own orchard. He also wanted to preserve open space by creating public squares, which still exist today. Penn's vision for a green Philadelphia created a lasting impact on the city. Philadelphia has acres upon acres of open space, known as Fairmount Park. And that foundation of instilling a love of nature in the early settlers to the city led to an innate curiosity about the natural world in residents of Philadelphia. Numerous naturalists claim roots in Philadelphia, including the Bartram family. As with other areas of society, Philadelphia also boasts many firsts with regard to the natural sciences.

The King's Botanist

JOHN BARTRAM WAS BORN on his family's farm in Darby, Pennsylvania, in 1699. There was nothing unique or special about his education, but from an early age he showed an inclination toward the study of botany and natural history. As an adult, he purchased 102 acres of land on the banks of the Schuylkill River. (At the time, the area was not part of Philadelphia, but it joined the city proper after consolidation.) The land was marshy, but Bartram decided to drain it and turn it into farmland. He was incredibly successful at growing crops and soon earned a reputation as a learned botanist. Bartram befriended Peter Collinson, a wealthy Quaker still living in England. Collinson tasked Bartram with sending seeds and plants of the New World back to Europe. Bartram is believed to have introduced some 200

William Bartram traveled the countryside to bring natural specimens back to Philadelphia.

(Engraving by unknown artist; via Wikimedia Commons, public domain)

A Beauty Saved from Extinction

DURING ONE OF THEIR EXCURSIONS in 1765, John and William Bartram came across a beautiful flowering tree growing in a small grove as they traveled along the Altamaha River in Georgia. The flower was a creamy white color with a glowing orange center.

William brought seeds from the tree back to the Bartram homestead in 1777 and named the tree *Franklinia,* in honor of Benjamin Franklin.

Somehow the tree became extinct in the wild, but the Bartrams still had the tree growing at their home. So they continued to cultivate it and essentially saved the tree, known scientifically as the *Franklinia altamaha,* from extinction.

Any *Franklinia* tree that grows now is descended from the seed the Bartrams brought back and saved from the wild.

John and William Bartram saved the *Franklinia* tree, with its creamy white blooms, from dying out.

(Illustration by William Bartram; via Wikimedia Commons, public domain)

PHILLY FACT Baltimore and Philadelphia have an ongoing fight over who has the right to Edgar Allan Poe. Baltimore might have his body, but Philadelphia can claim that the city was the place where he wrote much of his creative work. And the Edgar Allan Poe House is located in Philadelphia. A little-known piece of Poe's writing is a beautiful work of nature writing about the Wissahickon Valley Park. Poe published "Morning on the Wissahiccon" in 1843. Poe wrote:

A singular exemplification of my remarks upon this head may be found in the Wissahiccon, a brook, (for more it can scarcely be called,) which empties itself into the Schuylkill, about six miles westward of Philadelphia. Now the Wissahiccon is of so remarkable a loveliness that, were it flowing in England, it would be the theme of every bard, and the common topic of every tongue, if, indeed, its banks were not parcelled off in lots, at an exorbitant price, as building-sites for the villas of the opulent. Yet it is only within a very few years that any one has more than heard of the Wissahiccon, while the broader and more navigable water into which it flows, has been long celebrated as one of the finest specimens of American river scenery. The Schuylkill, whose beauties have been much exaggerated, and whose banks, at least in the neighbourhood of Philadelphia, are marshy like those of the Delaware, is not at all comparable, as an object of picturesque interest, with the more humble and less notorious rivulet of which we speak.

species native to America to Europe through his correspondence with Collinson. Bartram also set out to explore America outside of Philadelphia. He combed the country for new seeds and plants to bring back to his farm. In 1765, King George III named him "Royal Botanist in America." Bartram had become famous in America and England. Carolus Linnaeus (who came up with the system of binomial nomenclature for naming species) said Bartram was "the greatest natural botanist in the world." Bartram was also friends with Ben Franklin and helped found the American Philosophical Society.

Bartram's son William followed in his dad's footsteps by becoming a botanist and naturalist. William traveled across America to explore the natural history of the New World and gather plants, seeds, and other specimens. He became internationally famous, like his dad, and wrote extensively of his journeys in the southern part of the United States. His nature narrative, *Travels Through North and South Carolina, Georgia, East and West Florida, the Cherokee Country, the Extensive Territories of the Muscogulges or Creek Confederacy, and the Country of the Choctaws,* commonly known as *Travels,* is still considered a literary classic for nature lovers. Bartram's progeny also continued to run the farm and published the first catalog of American plants in 1783.

Today, Bartram's Garden is the oldest surviving botanical garden in North America. The estate changed ownership a few times over the years, with the City of Philadelphia purchasing the land in 1891. A nonprofit organization, the John Bartram Association, formed two years later to help the city take care of the site. The former homestead of the Bartrams is now a house museum and public historic garden open regularly for tours and exploration.

Naturally Speaking: Some Philadelphia Firsts

AS WE'VE SEEN IN OTHER CHAPTERS, Philadelphia has been the home for so many firsts—a number of them in the area of natural science. As early as the 1700s, Philadelphians had the idea of opening an American zoo. Travelers from exotic lands would often bring back animals to showcase for money. The idea really took hold, however, in the mid-1800s, when prominent doctor William Camac led the charge to establish America's first zoo. The Zoological Society of Philadelphia was born on March 21, 1859, but due to the raging Civil War, the zoo didn't open for business until 1874. On July 1 of that year, the zoo opened its beautiful Victorian gates, designed by well-known architect Frank Furness. The gates remain at the entrance to the zoo today, which is located in its original setting at 3400 Girard Avenue. The day the zoo opened, visitors came by foot, streetcar, horse and buggy, and steamboat to see the 813 animals. Admission was a mere quarter for adults and a dime for kids.

Today, the Philadelphia Zoo has more than 1,600 animals from 500 different species and hosts more than 1 million visitors each year.

Dinosaurs aren't necessarily what comes to mind when you hear the name Philadelphia, but where most of the dinosaurs live in the city leads to the next first. The Academy of Natural Sciences of Philadelphia (ANSP, now part of Drexel University) was founded in 1812 and remains the oldest natural-history research institute and museum in the country. The ANSP had some weighty competition when it began. Franklin and Bartram's American Philosophical Society was where all the cool intellectuals hung out. Nearby, Charles Willson Peale, a popular artist, had a museum with a huge collection of art, as well as artifacts from Lewis and Clark's expedition, along with shells, fossils, and other specimens. Some believe the founders of the ANSP started their museum because they weren't invited to join the American Philosophical Society. The founding members were Jacob Gilliams, Camillus MacMahon Mann, Nicholas Parmentier, Thomas Say, John Shinn, John Speakman, and Gerard Troost. Each was successful in his field but did not rise to the level of fame of Franklin or Bartram. The ANSP solely focused on the natural sciences, and the founding mission statement said it would be created "for the encouragement and cultivation of the sciences, and the advancement of useful learning." The ANSP charged explorers with the task of scouting out uncharted land in search of specimens, both plant and animal, to bring back for further examination. The doors to the ANSP officially opened in 1828, and its collection grew so quickly and consistently that it had to move its location several times before settling into its permanent home on 19th Street in 1876. Numerous notable scientists were affiliated in some way with the research institution, including John James Audubon and Charles Darwin. Bartram was an early member as well.

One of the notable leaders at the Academy of Natural Sciences was Joseph Leidy. Born in Philadelphia in 1823, Leidy studied medicine at the University of Pennsylvania, where he later became a professor of

Joseph Leidy was a Renaissance man when it came to the sciences, including forensics.

(Unknown photographer; via Wikimedia Commons, public domain)

anatomy. Leidy was involved in an event that would change the scope of natural-science exploration and discovery forever. In 1858, a hobby scientist named William Parker Foulke heard about some large bones that had been dug up some 20 years earlier in Haddonfield, New Jersey, a modern-day suburb of Philadelphia. Foulke gathered a crew together to dig and try to find more bones. What they discovered became the first nearly complete fossilized skeleton of a dinosaur. Leidy named the dinosaur specimen *Hadrosaurus foulkii* and posited that, given its structure, the dinosaur could have walked on two legs. His view was in opposition to the prevailing scientists of the day, but his theory would ultimately win out.

Leidy was accomplished in many different scientific areas, but he can claim one first as his own: He was the first person to ever use a microscope to solve a murder. In this day of CSI-style forensics, his discovery might seem inconsequential, but at the time, it was a remarkable feat. A Philadelphia farmer was dead, and the man suspected of committing the crime had blood on his clothes and his hatchet. The suspect had a ready explanation for the blood—he said it was from the chickens he had been slaughtering. Leidy didn't buy the theory and examined the blood under a microscope. He found that the blood evidence contained cells that could have only come from a human. The suspect ultimately confessed to the murder, and the case was closed. Forensics was born.

Leidy was greatly involved in the ANSP during his lifetime, serving as both the librarian and curator. He also served as the institution's president for the last 10 years of his life. Leidy helped organize and expand another science institution in the city, The Wagner Free Institute of Science. William Wagner had set out to offer scientific specimens and educational courses for free for anyone who was interested in the natural world. After Wagner's death, Leidy took over as president in 1885. Leidy died in 1891, but his legacy lives on. Today the Academy of Natural Sciences (otherwise known as "the dinosaur museum," given its displays) now boasts more than 18 million specimens in its collection and opens daily as a science museum for educational exploration.

Sowing Seeds

WHILE PHILADELPHIA WAS SOWING the seeds of a nation, metaphorically, some entrepreneurs were literally helping Americans sow seeds in their gardens. Two seed companies—the D. Landreth Seed Company and Burpee Home Gardens—were both born in Philadelphia. Philadelphia wasn't Landreth's first choice of location for his seed business; he actually chose Canada. Soon he discovered that Canada's harsh winter climate wasn't the best to propagate seeds. He decided to move to Philadelphia, given the city's reputation as a cultural hub. On January 7, 1784, Landreth opened his first garden center at 12th and High Streets (today's Market Street). He was so successful that he became a purveyor of seeds to every single president of the United States from Washington to Franklin D. Roosevelt. And, if you like potatoes and tomatoes, you have Landreth to thank for that. He introduced the first true white potato to the United States in 1811 and then followed nine years later by introducing the tomato, known then as the "love apple." He also introduced a favorite annual among gardeners: the zinnia, which came from Mexico.

Urban Farming

WHAT ONCE USED TO BE a wide, open green space quickly became a paved paradise. Farmland disappeared from Philadelphia and was replaced by factories, businesses, highways, and streets.

But in recent years, Philadelphia has seen resurgence in farming within the city limits. These farms, however, are not the traditional open pastures and fields that come to mind upon hearing the word farm. These new farms are an innovative use of smaller parcels of land.

The first of these urban farms in Philadelphia was the brainchild of a woman named Mary Seton Corboy. In the late 1990s, Corboy decided to take a small parcel of land in Kensington that was a former Superfund site and turn it into an urban green oasis.

These days, Greensgrow Farms has everything from farm animals (bees, chickens, and a pig) to farm-grown produce. They also have a nursery and run a CSA (Community Supported Agriculture) program in which people can get a weekly stash of fresh veggies and fruits from farms around Philadelphia.

The movement took flight after Greensgrow set down roots. Every year there are more urban farms popping up in every corner of the city.

Landreth and his son, David Landreth II, worked together to help form the Pennsylvania Horticultural Society (PHS) in 1828, America's first horticultural society. Two years later, PHS would host the very first indoor flower show, which, even to this day, is known as the granddaddy of all flower shows. The first Philadelphia Flower Show was held in the Masonic Temple on Chestnut Street and featured a new flower called the poinsettia. The show has since moved to the convention center and takes up 33 indoor acres; it hosts about 300,000 visitors each year.

Leading Ladies: The Haines Ladies

Jane Bowne Haines II started the Pennsylvania School of Horticulture for Women.

(Photo courtesy of Wyck Historic House, Garden, and Farm)

THE OLDEST HOUSE in the Germantown section of Philadelphia is called Wyck. It is also home to the oldest rose garden growing in its original design in the United States. The person to thank for that was a Quaker woman named Jane Bowne Haines. She was married to a man named Reuben Haines III. Reuben was a curious soul who was involved a bit in America's growing natural-science field. He was an early member of the Academy of Natural Sciences and served as its corresponding secretary.

When Jane married Reuben, she was a native New Yorker who was somewhat unhappy about moving to Philadelphia. She decided to focus much of her attention on turning the boring kitchen garden at the house into an amazing rose garden. Today, most of the roses at Wyck are still growing as they were planted more than 200 years ago and feature more than 30 different heirloom varieties.

Jane's granddaughter, Jane Bowne Haines II, carried on her grandmother's passion for horticulture by starting the Pennsylvania School of Horticulture for Women in 1910 in Ambler, a suburb of Philadelphia.

Today, the area of land where the school was located is part of Temple University's Ambler campus and offers several programs of horticultural study.

Wyck is now a historic home, rose garden, and urban farm.

The Landreth Seed Company is still in business, but it has had some struggles. In 2013, the company moved to New York and operates largely as a mail-order seed company. But each year you can still find Landreth seeds at the annual Flower Show.

Another Philadelphian also planted his company in Philadelphia and grew a seed empire. Washington Atlee Burpee was born in Philadelphia in 1858 and attended the grand Centennial exhibition as a curious 18-year-old. His parents hoped he would become a doctor, but young Burpee had other plans. Instead, he started a poultry and livestock mail-order company. He also dabbled in breeding and selling dogs, hogs, sheep, and goats, but legend has it that he started getting requests from clients for high-quality seeds because they missed the seeds they had back in Europe.

Burpee saw an opportunity to grow his business, literally and figuratively. By the 1880s, Burpee's seed business was booming, and it was supplying seeds to many parts of the new United States. Burpee found that many European varieties of seeds needed to become acclimated to American growing conditions, so he began crossing plants, creating the first hybrid vegetables in the New World. In 1888, he bought a farm in Doylestown, a suburb of Philadelphia, where he focused on improving seed quality for his growing client base. By 1915, Burpee was mailing out 1 million seed catalogs each year. The now-multimillion-dollar company is headquartered near Philadelphia in the suburb of Warminster. The Doylestown farm, Fordhook, still operates, and Burpee is now owned by George Ball Jr.

Hives and Scopes

IF YOU'VE EVER EATEN HONEY, you have Lorenzo Langstroth to thank. Langstroth was a Congregationalist minister who knew more about honeybees than anyone in the country. He was born in Philadelphia in 1810 and, as a child, he was always fascinated by insects. As an adult, he revisited this curiosity by focusing on the habits of honeybees. In

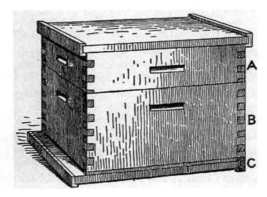

Lorenzo Langstroth (left) invented the Langstroth beehive, which had movable frames for gathering honey.

(Left: unknown photographer; right: illustration from Encyclopaedia Brittanica, *1911; both via Wikimedia Commons, public domain)*

1851, he designed a movable frame beehive that he patented a year later. His invention revolutionized beekeeping. Within 30 years, most beekeeping operations in the United States were using some form of the Langstroth Hive. Large-scale pollination operations relied on their honeybees to help proliferate crops. Langstroth's innovation earned him the title of "Father of American Beekeeping."

Another notable figure in natural science in this time period of Philadelphia was David Rittenhouse. A clockmaker and mathematician by trade, Rittenhouse started attracting attention when he observed the transit of the planet Venus in 1769. He was a member of the American Philosophical Society and took over as the APS president after Franklin's time leading the organization. Rittenhouse created a telescope, and he was believed to be one of the first, if not the first, to do so in the United States. He also got creative with spiderwebs, using them to create a system of crosshairs in telescopes. He was a Renaissance man who was active in numerous parts of Philadelphia society. He was the treasurer of Pennsylvania from 1777 to 1789 and was appointed the first director of the United States Mint under George Washington. He also was a prominent surveyor and helped draw the boundary lines for New Jersey, New York, Pennsylvania, and Maryland, among others. He was a quiet, unassuming man who didn't have many close friends; he was, however, quite close with Franklin and served as a pallbearer at Franklin's funeral.

Wide Open Spaces

WILLIAM PENN'S PLAN of Philadelphia containing a number of public open spaces was not lost on the generations that followed. When the cleanliness of the city's water supply became of paramount concern, the city moved forward to buy as much land as possible along the riverbanks of the Delaware and Schuylkill Rivers. That acquisition of land is how Fairmount Park *(see map on next page)* was born. The oldest part of Fairmount Park is the south garden at the Fairmount Water Works, which set down roots in 1829. A Philadelphia lawyer—Eli Kirk Price—was integral in acquiring the lands that make up today's 9,200 acres of Fairmount Park. Price was a real estate lawyer who was elected to the state senate in 1853, where his primary goal was to make the consolidation of Philadelphia happen. The Consolidation Act of 1854 was passed in February of that year and essentially tripled the size of the City of Brotherly Love. Price stepped down at the end of his senate term and worked on other efforts, including continuing his work on securing the land for Fairmount Park. The Fairmount Park Commission was created in 1867, and Price was one of its first commissioners. The Lemon Hill estate was added to Fairmount Park in 1855, and the park continued to grow over the years. The Wissahickon Valley was added in 1868, Cobbs Creek Park in 1904, Pennypack Park in 1905, and Tacony Creek Park in 1908. Penn's vision of his "greene countrie towne" forever became a reality because Philadelphia now contains one of the largest municipal urban parks in the country where natives and visitors regularly picnic, play, mountain bike, hike, and run.

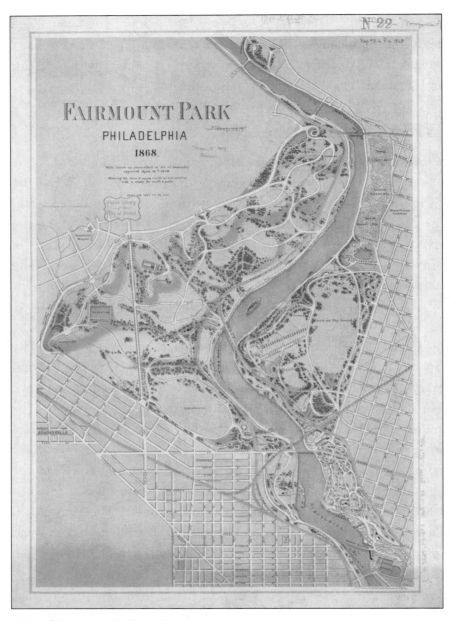

Map of Fairmount Park, 1868

CHAPTER 7

CANVASSING THE CITY

ONE OF THE MOST ICONIC BUILDINGS IN PHILADELPHIA is the majestic Philadelphia Museum of Art, rising mightily above the banks of the Schuylkill River near Fairmount Dam. As the art scene in Philadelphia was setting up shop, so too were modern buildings designed by renowned architects, an equally iconic parkway, publishing powerhouses, and a reimagined city center. William Penn's city would take its love of art, architecture, and words to new levels as the city continued to grow.

In the mid-1800s, city planners decided that Philadelphia needed a grand boulevard to connect the city with its suburbs. But it wasn't until 1891 that the idea came to fruition. That year, the city council received a proposal accompanied by a petition requesting the construction of a 160-foot-wide road connecting Center City to the rapidly growing Fairmount Park. A year later, the council would unanimously

The Ben Franklin Parkway is a majestic street between City Hall and the art museum.

(Photo: Dave Tavani)

pass a bill to construct the "Fairmount Parkway," known today as the Benjamin Franklin Parkway. Years went by, however, before ground was broken in 1907, followed by more years of getting nowhere with construction. In 1917, the Fairmount Park Commission accepted a design from Jacques Gréber, an urban designer. In the plan, Logan Square became the center from which the new parkway was anchored. Parkway construction was under way.

Elements of what we think of as quintessential Philadelphia started popping up around the parkway. The Swann Memorial Fountain, named for Philadelphia Fountain Society founder Dr. Wilson Cary Swann, came into existence in 1924 and is the focal point of Logan Square. Renowned sculptor Alexander Calder was the designer and left his mark all over the city. (More on him later.) The city completed the parkway in 1926, and in 1937 the parkway officially changed its name to honor its most beloved Philadelphian, Benjamin Franklin. In 1927, the main branch of the Philadelphia Library opened, designed by Horace Trumbauer. A year later, the first section of the Philadelphia Museum of Art opened at the helm of the parkway.

Temple of the Arts

THE PHILADELPHIA MUSEUM OF ART (PMA) did not originate in the stately home where it now stands. It actually arose from the Centennial Exhibition of 1876 (see page 68), the big party Philadelphia hosted to celebrate 100 years of freedom. Memorial Hall, which today houses the Please Touch Museum, was created as the art gallery for the centennial, displaying more than 4,000 pieces. After the party's conclusion, the building stayed open for a few decades and showcased decorative arts as well as industrial instruments. The collection continued to grow, and as wealthy people died, they began leaving their art collections to the museum. It was soon clear that the museum needed more space.

> **PHILLY FACT** There are 72 steps leading up to the Philadelphia Museum of Art. The steps gained fame when fictional Philadelphian Rocky Balboa used them in his training routine. Tourists and natives alike can often be seen running to the top of the steps and raising their arms in victory, Rocky-style. There's even a statue of Rocky near the steps where tourists line up every day for photo ops.

The proposal to erect the art museum atop Fairmount, at the city's second highest natural elevation point, came in 1907. With the completion of City Hall at one end of the Fairmount Parkway in 1901, the new art museum would serve as a bookend on the other side of the parkway. The plan for the PMA was finalized in 1917 and came together from the work of several architects. The architecture firm of Zantzinger, Borie & Medary, along with Paul Cret and Horace Trumbauer's firm, all had a hand in the design. However, Julian Abele, senior designer at the Trumbauer firm, was the chief designer of the new museum. Abele was the first African American to graduate from the University of Pennsylvania's architecture program.

The building officially opened in 1928 and took on the form of three connected Greek temples. The building had opened in sections, under pressure from the estates of William Elkins, George Elkins, and John H. McFadden. All three wills stated that the museum could have their substantial art collections as long as there was a "suitable" place

The templelike Philadelphia Museum of Art (left), with the
Fairmount Water Works in the foreground

(Photo: Dave Tavani)

for the display of the art within a reasonable amount of time after
their deaths. Because the museum didn't want to lose the paintings, it
opened temporary galleries to meet the guidelines of the estates.

One of the earliest great collectors of art in Philadelphia was John
G. Johnson, whom we read about in Chapter 3. Johnson was an attorney and an avid art collector. Over his lifetime, he amassed a collection
of more than 1,300 works of art. He displayed them at his home on
South Broad Street, and as he aged, he decided he wanted the art to
find a distinguished home in which to be displayed. He was a member
of the Fairmount Park Commission and knew that the construction
of the art museum was on the horizon. He feared, however, that the
museum would never come to fruition. So instead, he purchased 510
S. Broad St. to house and exhibit his paintings. In his final will and tes-
tament, he bequeathed his collection to the City of Philadelphia, under

the condition that the city agree to continue to exhibit his collection at the Broad Street location. The city, however, had other plans. In 1921, it asked the orphans' court permission to sell 510 S. Broad and use the money earned to help fund the building of the new art museum. The petition was denied.

Then, in 1933, the Johnson collection was housed in the art museum temporarily. A whopping 100,000 people came to see the collection that year. Twenty-one years later, Johnson's estate asked the court to allow the collection to be displayed at the art museum permanently. After some legal wrangling, the court agreed, but it required the trustees to check in with the court every 10 years. In 1989, the court said the Johnson collection could remain at the PMA until December 31, 2083.

Today's PMA—the third-largest art museum in the country—contains 80 period rooms and holds more than a quarter-million works of art and artifacts in its collections.

Early Artists

NOW WE NEED TO BACK UP a bit in history to understand the foundation of Philadelphia as a city of art and look at some of the early artists who called Philadelphia home. Although he wasn't born in Philadelphia, Charles Willson Peale adopted Philadelphia as his home in 1775, at the dawn of the Revolutionary War. He painted war heroes and portraits of founding fathers, including John Adams, Ben Franklin, Thomas Jefferson, and George Washington. He also founded the first major museum in America, called Peale's Museum, which focused on natural history and artifacts.

Peale was pivotal in the development of the oldest art museum and art school in the country—the Pennsylvania Academy of the Fine Arts (PAFA). Peale, along with an artist widely considered the first significant American sculptor, William Rush, founded PAFA in 1805 with the idea that the organization would become both an academy to educate artists and a repository to exhibit art. Since its inception, PAFA has been a world-renowned art institution and continues to operate

Charles Willson Peale helped found the Pennsylvania Academy of the Fine Arts (right).

(Left: self-portrait by Charles Willson Peale; right: unknown photographer; both via Wikimedia Commons, public domain)

as both a school and museum. The collection at PAFA is installed in chronological and thematic order to showcase the evolution of American art and artists.

One of the most well-known early students at PAFA was an artist who was largely rejected by both the public and his fellow artists. Thomas Eakins was born in Philadelphia in 1844 and spent nearly his entire life in Philadelphia. He attended PAFA right after high school and took anatomy classes at Jefferson Medical College at the same time. His style was focused on realism and capturing the beauty in everyday life. One of his most famous paintings, *The Gross Clinic,* hangs today in the Philadelphia Museum of Art. It depicts a surgery, and for the time period in which it was painted, it was considered quite shocking. Eakins sold only 30 paintings in his lifetime but posthumously gained favor in the art establishment as one of America's best painters. Eakins died in 1916, and today thousands of people drive around Eakins Oval, a roundabout named in his honor, at the foot of the art museum's steps.

On the opposite end of the Benjamin Franklin Parkway stands Logan Square, adorned with the Swann Fountain. Artist Alexander Stirling

Painter Thomas Eakins gained artistic acclaim after his death.

(Self-portrait by Thomas Eakins; via Wikimedia Commons, public domain)

Calder designed the fountain at the center of the park, which is also commonly called Logan Circle due to its use as a traffic circle. Calder was a member Philadelphia's first family of sculptors. Calder's father, Alexander Milne, was also a noted sculptor who had the honor of creating the bronze sculpture of William Penn that sits high atop City Hall. The younger Calder designed three Native American sculptures at the Swann Fountain representing the major bodies of water in Philadelphia: Wissahickon Creek, the Schuylkill River, and the Delaware River. The youngest artist in the Calder family, Alexander Calder (a.k.a. Sandy), also has an abstract sculpture along the Ben Franklin Parkway. His claim to fame is that he invented the mobile and is said to have transformed the notion of modern sculpture. His mobile *Ghost,* which often appears to be floating in midair, is permanently displayed in the Great Stair Hall at the PMA. Today, Calder sculptures from all three generations are considered iconic works of art.

Building the City

PHILADELPHIA IS A CITY filled with amazing architecture. Books can be and have been written about the beauty, history, and artisanship of many of the famous architects who called Philadelphia home. We'll focus on a few of the biggies from the early days of building the city from scratch.

First and foremost is the man believed to be the first professional architect in the country, Benjamin Henry Latrobe. We met Latrobe back in Chapter 2 when we discussed his work on the Fairmount

Alexander Stirling Calder designed the Swann Fountain at Logan Square.

(Photo: © Jared Kofsky, PlaceNJ.com/Wikimedia Commons/CC-BY-SA 3.0)

Water Works system. Latrobe was born in England and found his way to Philadelphia in 1798. Even though he was not a native, he considered Philadelphia to be his home. Latrobe's first major project was the Bank of Pennsylvania, which was the first major building project in America to be in the Greek Revival style. The building was unfortunately demolished in 1870. His most significant accomplishment on the national level was the design of the US Capitol in Washington, D.C.

One of Latrobe's assistants, William Strickland, also earned a reputation as a master architect in Philadelphia and the nation. Strickland was born in New Jersey in 1788, but his family moved to Philadelphia two years later. As a young man, Strickland landed a job working on the Bank of Pennsylvania, and Latrobe agreed to take him on as an apprentice. Strickland's first major contract was to design the Masonic Hall in Philadelphia in 1808. He went on to win other major architectural competitions in the city, including the Second Bank of the United

William Strickland's architecture helped shape Philadelphia.

(Painting by John Neagle; via Wikimedia Commons, public domain)

States, the US Mint building in Philadelphia, and the US Naval Asylum. Outside of the Philadelphia area, Strickland's biggest accomplishment was the Tennessee State Capitol in Nashville.

One of Strickland's competitors and contemporaries was John Haviland. Born in England, Haviland found his way to Philadelphia in 1816. His first major commission was the First Presbyterian Church in 1820. He earned many major projects throughout the next few years, including the design of Eastern State Penitentiary and the Franklin Institute. Haviland was not so good at managing his money, however, and he found himself bankrupt and without major commissions in his later life.

One of Philadelphia's most iconic buildings is its City Hall, located in Center City in what Penn deemed his "Center Square." It was always William Penn's intention that his City of Brotherly Love would be run from where City Hall now sits, but early development in the city was mostly along the Delaware River. When it came time to build a new home for the city's central government, however, the intersection of Broad and Market Streets won. Planning started in 1870, and the city chose Scottish architect John McArthur Jr. to design its new central office building; McArthur hired Thomas Ustick Walter, who had previously designed Girard College, to be his assistant in the City Hall project. The architecture is elaborate and is in the style known as French Second Empire. The design was controversial from the beginning because people wondered what such a highly adorned building

Leading Ladies: Cecilia Beaux and Sara Worthington Peter

ONE OF THE MOST IMPORT- ANT ARTISTS to come out of Philadelphia was Cecilia Beaux. Born in Philadelphia on May 1, 1855, she had a tough beginning in life when her mother died 12 days after giving birth. Beaux's father then left her and her older sister in the care of relatives when he returned to France.

Portraitist Cecilia Beaux was one of Philadelphia's foremost early female artists.

(Unknown photographer; via Wikimedia Commons, public domain)

was doing in a Quaker city. The building withstood the test of time and avoided several threats of demolition.

City Hall has more than 250 sculptures both inside and out, all designed by Alexander Milne Calder. The most well known of his sculptures at City Hall is, of course, the gigantic statue of William Penn that rises 548 feet above the city. When McArthur designed the building, he intended it to be the tallest building in the world. But it would have competition from the beginning, finally losing out to

Beaux had an early interest in art and by the age of 18 was making money as a commercial artist. In 1885, her portrait of her sister and nephew, titled *Last Days of Infancy,* was exhibited at the Pennsylvania Academy of Fine Art. She studied in Europe for more than a year and then returned to Philadelphia.

In 1895, she became the first female instructor at PAFA, and she garnered wide success as a portrait painter. In 1900, she moved to New York and then later to Massachusetts, where she died in 1942.

Throughout her lifetime, Beaux earned a reputation as one of the best portrait painters in America during the late 1800s and early 1900s. She won numerous awards and was even honored by First Lady Eleanor Roosevelt in 1933.

Another leading lady in the Philadelphia art world was Sara Worthington Peter. Although she was born in Ohio, she spent some time in Philadelphia in the 1840s where she met and married her second husband, William Peter. In 1848, she founded the Philadelphia School of Design for Women, which today is Moore College of Art & Design. The school's mission was to help women learn the craft of drawing and design so they could support themselves and contribute to the manu-facturing community at large.

New York City's Metropolitan Life Building in 1909. Before that, the Eiffel Tower and the Washington Monument both rose above the height of City Hall, but since neither was a "true" building, City Hall kept its tallest title for a short time. McArthur's City Hall wouldn't see its way to completion until 1901, some 30 years after construc-tion began. Although there was never an official statement, there was a "gentleman's agreement" that no building should ever be built taller than William Penn's hat atop City Hall. Builders honored that

Philadelphia's City Hall sits where William Penn had hoped the center of his town would be.

(Photo: Dave Tavani)

agreement for decades until the construction of Liberty Place broke it in 1987. Since then, skyscrapers have towered over William Penn. And if you're superstitious, you might believe that Penn was none too happy about the breaking of the agreement (see "The Curse of William Penn," Chapter 9, page 145).

City Hall is the largest municipal building in the country, with a whopping 700 rooms. It is home to all three branches of Philadelphia's government and is open regularly for tours.

Another giant who looms large in Philadelphia's early architecture scene is Frank Furness. He was born in Philadelphia in 1839, and even though he didn't attend college, he was wildly successful. He was an officer in the Civil War and received a Congressional Medal of Honor. He designed numerous mansions for the wealthy of Philadelphia; Chicago; Washington, D.C.; and New York. One of his major accomplishments, however, was his commission as chief architect of Reading Railroad. He also designed for the Pennsylvania and B&O Railroads, including numerous stations throughout Philadelphia and Delaware. In addition, he designed the First Unitarian Church of Philadelphia, the Pennsylvania Academy of the Fine Arts building, and the Girard Trust Company in Center City, which is today the Ritz-Carlton hotel. He went on to design more than 600 buildings before his death in 1912. He's buried in Philadelphia's Laurel Hill Cemetery.

The Written Word

WHILE PHILADELPHIA IS NOT the city that usually comes to mind when thinking about a publishing Mecca, the written word did have its heyday in the city's early history. Since Philadelphia enjoyed being the cultural and financial center of the Americas in its early years, it's no surprise that it was the publishing center as well. However, it quickly lost that title to New York and never recovered it.

J. B. Lippincott Company was an early publisher in Philadelphia. The company got its start from a tiny print shop and bookstore in 1792. A man named Jacob Johnson started it and eventually sold it to John Grigg, who in turn focused on medical publishing. In 1830, the company published Dr. Samuel Gross's *Anatomy, Physiology and Diseases of the Bones and Joints.* J. B. Lippincott bought the company from Grigg in 1850 and made the company incredibly profitable. It published popular fiction, including Harper Lee's classic, *To Kill a Mockingbird.* The company has changed hands a number of times and today exists as Lippincott Williams & Wilkins (LWW), a division of the Amsterdam-based publishing conglomerate Wolters Kluwer. LWW publishes numerous medical and trade publications and employs hundreds of people.

One of the earliest publishing empires in Philadelphia came after the city had lost its powerhouse title to New York. Enter Cyrus H. K. Curtis. Curtis was born in Maine in 1850 and spent his early career in Boston. He later moved to Philadelphia and started a publication called *Tribune and Farmer,* a magazine focusing on agriculture. Curtis had the idea of including a page in the publication dedicated to women. When his wife, Louise Knapp, saw the content, however, she was amused by his failed attempt to figure out what women would like to read. Curtis told his wife to give it a try, and her column was hugely successful. In fact, it was so popular that Curtis decided to sell

Cyrus Curtis was the head of a publishing empire in Philadelphia.

(Unknown photographer; via Wikimedia Commons, public domain)

his part of *Tribune and Farmer* and start a new publication called *Ladies' Home Journal* in 1883. By 1900, it was the first American magazine to reach a million subscribers.

When Curtis died in 1933, *Ladies' Home Journal* had more than 2.5 million subscribers. With his early success, Curtis decided to start the Curtis Publishing Company in 1891. He would later go on to buy *The Saturday Evening Post* and turn it into one of the most popular magazines in American history. In 1961, *The Saturday Evening Post* was selling 7 million copies a week. Curtis became one of the wealthiest men in the country and shared his fortune through philanthropy. His daughter, Mary Louise Curtis Bok, later founded the Curtis Institute of Music in 1924 with funding from her father. His daughter also turned Curtis's country estate, located just outside city limits, into an arboretum to honor her father.

One well-known publishing name in Philadelphia is not that of a native son. Walter Annenberg was born in Wisconsin and came to

Philadelphia in 1927 to attend the Wharton School at the University of Pennsylvania. He left after only one year to join his father's media company, Triangle Publications. Annenberg went on to own and sell *The Philadelphia Inquirer* and *Philadelphia Daily News.* He also started the incredibly popular *TV Guide* in Philadelphia. Annenberg's name is well known these days mainly because of the Annenberg Foundation, a philanthropic organization. In addition, the communication schools at the University of Pennsylvania and the University of Southern California bear Annenberg's name.

The Father of Modern Philadelphia

THE STRUCTURE AND RHYTHM of today's Philadelphia is largely due to the work of noted city planner Edmund Bacon. Often called "The Father of Modern Philadelphia," Bacon was a native Philadelphian who studied architecture at Cornell University. He was a staff member at the Philadelphia Planning Commission in 1947 when he worked on the Better Philadelphia Exhibition. The exhibit was a showcase of what Philadelphia could be, given the right redevelopment. Nearly 400,000 people visited the exhibition at Gimbel's Department Store at Eighth and Market Streets to see what Philadelphia could become. Soon afterward, Bacon became the executive director of the City Planning Commission and served in that role for 21 years. During his tenure, the city underwent a transformation. He is credited with the redevelopment of Society Hill, which was once a run-down, ugly part of the city, quite contrary to the wealthy, manicured neighborhood it is today. Bacon also oversaw the development of Independence Mall, Market East, Penn's Landing, Penn Center, University City, and parts of the Far Northeast. He worked with architect Vincent G. King to design one of the most iconic spots in Philadelphia: LOVE Park. Officially known as JFK Plaza, LOVE Park was built in 1965 as the bookend to the Benjamin Franklin Parkway.

Bacon believed that Philadelphia could become a world-class city and that effective design could reattract middle-class families who had

The City of Philadelphia Mural Arts Program honored city planner Edmund Bacon with a mural in Center City painted by street artist Gaia.

(The Father of Modern Philadelphia, © 2013 City of Philadelphia Mural Arts Program/Gaia; photo: Steve Weinik)

previously fled the city. He was once asked what his greatest accomplishment was, and he replied simply, "Philadelphia." He is also well known as the father of actor Kevin Bacon, but his accomplishments stand well on their own merits. He was even featured on the cover of *Time* magazine in 1964 because of his visionary abilities to move Philadelphia forward. He died in 2005, but his legacy lives on in every corner of today's Philadelphia.

The Benjamin Franklin Parkway also plays a prominent role in today's Philadelphia. The stately parkway is lined with flags from every nation in the world and has become home to major concerts and events. In 2015, the parkway hosted Pope Francis, who conducted a Mass for more than a million people. And its safe to say that since Bacon's tenure, the city has steadily been undergoing continued growth—imperceptible at times but steadfast at others.

City of Murals

IN THE 1980s, Philadelphia had a graffiti problem. It was every-where, and most people thought it was pretty darned ugly. In 1984, the Philadelphia Anti-Graffiti Network was created to combat the scourge of graffiti across the city. The organization hired an artist named Jane Golden to lead the charge.

The mission statement of the program was, and still is, "Art ignites change." The idea was to hire artists to create public murals to cover graffiti and beautify the city at the same time. Another idea was that people would be less likely to create graffiti over a work of art.

The program was incredibly successful and has earned Philadelphia the nickname "City of Murals." In 1996, the program morphed into the City of Philadelphia Mural Arts Program, and Jane Golden is still at the helm.

Each year, the organization helps create between 50 and 100 public murals, employing approximately 150 artists in the process.

Philadelphia is also now home to the second largest mural in the world. *How Philly Moves,* located at Philadelphia International Airport, takes up a whopping 85,000 square feet.

Since its inception, the Mural Arts Program has created more than 3,600 murals.

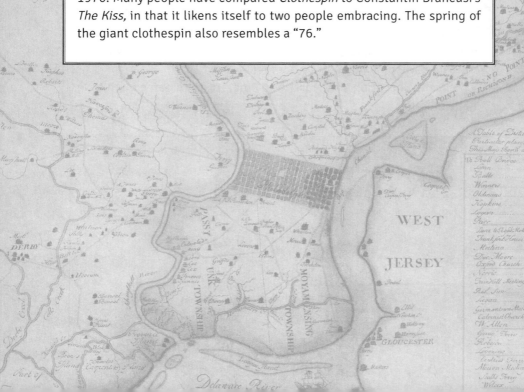

Looming Large

TWO OF THE MOST ICONIC WORKS of art in Philadelphia are both in the center of the city. The LOVE statue, in LOVE Park (JFK Plaza), draws locals and natives who pose for photos in front of it.

Pop artist Robert Indiana designed the image that would evolve into the LOVE statue in 1967, when the Metropolitan Museum of Art asked him to design a Christmas card. Indiana didn't bother to copyright the image at the time because he didn't think too much of it. The popularity of the image, however, exploded and began showing up everywhere.

The LOVE statue arrived in Philadelphia in 1976 for the city's Bicentennial celebration. It left briefly but came back to stay in 1978.

Another hugely iconic sculpture, both literally and figuratively, is *Clothespin*, by Claes Oldenburg. The 45-foot steel clothespin stands directly across the street from City Hall. It also arrived in Philadelphia in 1976. Many people have compared *Clothespin* to Constantin Brancusi's *The Kiss,* in that it likens itself to two people embracing. The spring of the giant clothespin also resembles a "76."

LOVE Park

(Photo: © M. Fischetti/Visit Philadelphia)

~ CHAPTER 8 ~

THE SOUND OF PHILADELPHIA

WHILE PHILADELPHIA'S EARLIEST SOUNDS were often in the form of religious music, the later years of the City of Brotherly Love saw remarkable contributions to American jazz culture and the spread of rock 'n' roll.

Geographically speaking, in the 1900s Philadelphia was situated across the river from the country's largest maker of music in Camden, New Jersey. But even before that, Philadelphia hosted the unveiling of Emile Berliner's gramophone, which was in competition with Thomas Edison's phonograph. The Berliner Gramophone Company had an office and factory in Philadelphia and even opened the nation's first record store at 1237 Chestnut St. The company had some money problems and ended up selling out to Eldridge Johnson, who owned a machine shop

Marian Anderson was one of the most celebrated singers of her time.

(Photo: Carl Van Vechten; via Wikimedia Commons, public domain)

in Camden. Johnson created the Victor Talking Machine Company in 1901. He moved his recording studio to 10th Street in Philadelphia while production at its Camden factory ballooned. Philadelphia musicians had easy access to Victor and recorded a young woman named Marian Anderson, one of the greatest musicians ever to come out of Philadelphia.

Anderson was born in Philadelphia on February 27, 1897. As a young child, she showed talent as a singer, but her family couldn't afford to obtain formal music training for her. At age 6, she joined the choir at Union Baptist Church and spent a great deal of time singing and practicing for the choir. Her church was so impressed with her commitment that members pooled together $500 so Anderson could study and train under noted voice instructor Giuseppe Boghetti. Anderson's career then was nearly unstoppable, although she would hit racial roadblocks along the way. In 1925, she sang with the New York Philharmonic Orchestra; two years later, she performed at Carnegie Hall. She toured throughout Europe and the United States and had the honor of being invited to perform at the White House for President Franklin D. Roosevelt and his wife, Eleanor. Anderson was the first African American ever to perform at the White House.

Anderson continued to break barriers. In 1955, she became the first African American to perform as a member of the New York Metropolitan

Famous Musicians from Philadelphia

PHILADELPHIA HAS ITS SHARE of famous musicians who have called the city their home. Here's a short list of famous Philadelphia music stars that is by no means comprehensive. There are simply too many to name!

- **Bessie Smith** (1894–1937) was a legendary blues singer who was born in Tennessee but made Philadelphia her home in 1923. She is often referred to as the "Empress of the Blues." She is considered one of the preeminent singers of her time.

- **Mario Lanza** (1921–1959) was a tenor and movie heartthrob who sang in operas and starred in Hollywood musicals. He sold millions of albums.

- **Stan Getz** (1927–1991) was a jazz saxophonist. He was born in Philadelphia but moved to New York early in his life.

- **Daryl Hall** and **John Oates** met in 1967 and realized they were both students at Temple University. As Hall & Oates, they've sold millions of albums and have had numerous number-one hits. They were inducted into the Rock and Roll Hall of Fame in 2014.

- **Patti LaBelle** is an R&B superstar. Before going solo, she was in a group called The Blue Belles, later renamed Patti LaBelle and the Bluebelles. The 1970s incarnation, Labelle—Patti LaBelle, Sarah Dash, and Nona Hendryx—was the first African American vocal group to both perform at the Metropolitan Opera House and grace the cover of *Rolling Stone*.

- **Jill Scott** is an R&B and soul singer born and raised in Philadelphia. She grew up in North Philadelphia and went to Temple University. Her debut album sold more than 1 million copies.

- **G-Love** is the lead singer of the hip-hop/blues band G. Love and Special Sauce. Born Garrett Dutton, G-Love is a Philadelphia favorite who helped acoustic rocker Jack Johnson get discovered (Johnson appeared on the band's 1999 album *Philadelphonic*).

- **Boyz II Men** is an R&B group that got its start in 1985 with a group of students at Philadelphia High School for the Creative and Performing Arts (CAPA). The original members were George Baldi, Nathan Morris, Marc Nelson, Jon Shoats, and Marguerite Walker. Joining later were Michael McCary, Wanya Morris, and Shawn Stockman. The group shattered records in the 1990s, and their songs spent a collective 50 weeks at *Billboard's* number-one spot.

- **DJ Jazzy Jeff and the Fresh Prince** were a hip-hop duo from West Philadelphia. Jeff Townes and Will Smith hit the scene in the late 1980s and early 1990s with their Grammy Award–winning hits "Parents Just Don't Understand" and "Summertime," Philadelphia's anthem of summer. Will Smith later went on to TV and movie fame.

- **The Roots** are a Philadelphia favorite. The hip-hop/neo-soul band started in 1987 when founding members Tariq "Black Thought" Trotter and Ahmir "Questlove" Thompson were also students at CAPA. They are currently the house band on *The Tonight Show with Jimmy Fallon.*

Opera. In 1939, when her manager tried to book a performance for her at Washington, D.C.'s Constitution Hall, she was denied. The owners of the hall, the Daughters of the American Revolution, told Anderson's manager that there were no dates available. Word got out, though, that the DAR had a policy that forbade African Americans from performing at the hall. When Eleanor Roosevelt found out about this act of discrimination, she dropped her DAR membership and invited Anderson to perform at the Lincoln Memorial on Easter Sunday. Thousands attended the concert, which was also broadcast for millions to see across the nation. Anderson's voice shattered the racial walls that had been put in her way, and she paved the way for future black performers.

In 1961, Anderson sang the national anthem at President John F. Kennedy's inauguration. Kennedy later honored her with the Presidential Medal of Freedom. In 1991, she received a Grammy Award for Lifetime Achievement. She died in 1993, but the recordings of her voice and the trails that she blazed will forever live on. Her life and legacy are honored at the Marian Anderson Residence Museum, located at 762 S. Martin St. in Center City West.

The Music Bureau

WITH ALL OF THE FUNDING CUTS that are so common among the arts, it's a wonder that during the Great Depression Philadelphia had its own government department for music. Called the Municipal Music Bureau of Philadelphia, the agency was started in 1929 by Mayor Harry Mackey. It was part of the Department of Public Welfare and was the first such department in the country. Heading the bureau was Clara Barnes Abbott. The purpose of the bureau was to make Philadelphia a city of music, providing music festivals, concerts, and information about music to residents across the city. The organization also saw to the installation of about 3,000 radios in hospitals, playgrounds, and other public spaces throughout the city. There was even a special "municipal music car" that would drive around the city, park in a neighborhood, and try to start an instant dance party. People loved the Music Bureau, but alas, its existence was short-lived. Economic troubles closed the bureau in 1933, silencing the roving dance parties and regular concerts.

All That Jazz

AFTER THE END OF WORLD WAR I and throughout much of the early 20th century, Philadelphia saw an increase in the number of African Americans who came to call the city their home. It's no coincidence that at the same time, the sound of jazz was taking over Philadelphia and creating a legacy. Throughout the 1940s, 1950s, and 1960s, the city saw the opening of more than 30 jazz clubs, many of which were located in North Philadelphia. The names of jazz legends either born in Philadelphia or who spent a great deal of time living and playing there is a veritable who's who of jazz history: John Coltrane, Stan Getz, Dizzy Gillespie, Billie Holiday (see sidebar on page 134), Charlie Parker, and Bessie Smith, among others. Some of the famous clubs to host jazz music included Pep's and the Clef Club.

John Coltrane may have one of the longest-standing legacies in the city. Although he was born in North Carolina in 1926, he moved to Philadelphia in 1943 to try and make it as a professional musician. But the country was at war, and Coltrane ended up serving in the Navy band in Hawaii before returning to Philadelphia in 1946. Coltrane started making a name for himself and joined several famous bands led by jazz legends including Dizzy Gillespie and Miles Davis. Coltrane, unfortunately, had developed an addiction to heroin, and his dabbling in drugs led to his firing. Coltrane did end up beating his addiction and decided to strike out on his own as a soloist. His style was unique and experimental, marked partly by the way he could play several notes on his saxophone at the same time. His biggest album, *A Love Supreme*, came out in 1965 and earned him two Grammy awards. Coltrane died young in 1967 from liver cancer. The home Coltrane lived in on Thirty-Third Street from 1952 to 1958 is now a National Historic Landmark. Coltrane was awarded a lifetime-achievement Grammy posthumously in 1992.

Mummers!

YOU CAN'T TALK ABOUT MUSIC in Philadelphia without talking about the Mummers. Native Philadelphians either love or hate the Mummers—there's really no in between. Mummers are men (and now women) dressed in feathers, sequins, and exquisite costumery, usually wearing makeup and golden slippers, who play in string bands, perform skits, and strut their stuff every New Year's Day.

The annual Mummers Parade is Philadelphia at its core. Thousands turn out each January 1 to watch the parade and celebrate the arrival of a new year. There are five divisions of the Mummers: the Comics, the Fancies, the Wench Brigades, the String Bands, and the Fancy Brigades. Those involved in the Mummers often have deep familial roots in their organizations that go back many generations. Mummers also have a strong working-class heritage.

Mummery goes back centuries to many parts of Europe. When folks started arriving in Philadelphia from Scandinavia, Britain, and other parts of Europe, they brought mummery with them. "To mum" means to mime, mask, or play. Historically, to mum is also to make fun of the leading class and to ask for food or drink.

Back in the old days, people would bring firearms to the Mummers Parade, which officially dates back to 1901. People would shoot their guns into the air to celebrate. Bringing guns was eventually outlawed, but the full name of the parade's official museum is the New Year's Shooters and Mummers Museum.

The Mummers Parade is the oldest continuous folk parade in the country—and truly Philadelphian.

Mummers are a New Year's Day tradition in Philadelphia.

The explosion of the jazz era would evolve into bebop and later doo-wop, and although not the center of the movement, Philadelphia hosted musicians in the new and growing genre. But it would all eventually take a backseat to the hot, new music trend hitting the airwaves of the city and the country: rock 'n' roll. And once rock 'n' roll took hold, it never let go. Enter *American Bandstand*.

"Where Things Are Poppin' the Philadelphia Way"

ROCK 'N' ROLL HAS STRONG ROOTS in Philadelphia. Some say rock music started here. That's debatable, but what's for sure is that a number of teenage heartthrobs and rock icons of the 1950s and 1960s came from the City of Brotherly Love, including Frankie Avalon, Chubby Checker, James Darren, Fabian, and Bobby Rydell. And they all got their chance to perform on the most happening television show around, *American Bandstand*.

Bandstand started in Philadelphia as a local show in 1952. The host was DJ Bob Horn, and it was filmed at 46th and Market Streets in a room called Studio B. The show featured local teens dancing to the hottest hits on the airwaves. It was insanely popular across the Delaware Valley. Then a young chap named Dick Clark took over the show in 1956, right before it began broadcasting to a national audience. The show came on every weekday right as kids were getting home from school, and its popularity across the country exploded, regularly reaching about 20 million viewers. Local teenagers would line up for blocks around the studio to try to get their chance to dance on *Bandstand.* Some of the regulars even became famous nationwide.

Bandstand called Philadelphia its home until 1962, when it moved out to Hollywood. At that time, the show frequency changed to only once a week. The show broadcast its final season in 1989. It made the career of the legendary Dick Clark and secured Philly's role in rock 'n' roll history.

American Bandstand got its start in Philadelphia. City youth used to clamor for tickets so they could be part of the show.

(Photo: WFIL-TV/ABC/Click Corporation; via Wikimedia Commons, public domain)

Sounds of Soul

THE MUSIC COMING OUT OF PHILADELPHIA quickly had competition from the sounds coming out of the Motor City and some Brits across the pond. Motown took center stage in the early 1960s, and the Beatles started the British invasion that would take America by storm.

Philadelphia would reemerge onto the music scene, though, in the late 1960s and early 1970s not with music performers, but with two behind-the-scenes guys who eventually opened a music studio that created the new Sound of Philadelphia. Camden, New Jersey, native Leon Huff and Philadelphia native Kenny Gamble were songwriters and producers. Sigma Sound Studio opened up shop at 212 N. 12th St. and was run by Thom Bell and Joe Tarsia. Then in 1971, Columbia Records signed a deal with Gamble and Huff to start their own music label called Philadelphia International Records. Gamble and Huff would write and produce the music and record at Sigma Sound. During the 1970s and early 1980s, Gamble and Huff were on fire. They produced and recorded more than 170 gold and platinum albums. Some of their talent included Harold Melvin and the Bluenotes, the O'Jays, and Wilson Pickett. They also went on to write "The Sound of Philadelphia," which would become the theme song for the wildly popular television show *Soul Train.* Some of their other popular songs include "Love Train" by the O'Jays, "When Will I See You Again?" by The Three Degrees, and "I'm Gonna Make You Love Me" by Dee Dee Warren (later covered by Diana Ross and the Supremes as well as The Temptations).

As music changed, so did the popularity of records. Gamble and Huff's label closed up shop in 2001, but the Sound of Philadelphia still lives on over the airwaves and in digital form.

A different sound of Philadelphia would emerge from the Philadelphia Orchestra. The orchestra was founded in 1900 but didn't gain national and international prestige until Leopold Stokowski took over as conductor in 1912. He would bring the orchestra all the way to Hollywood to showcase their musical talents to perform the music of the Disney movie *Fantasia.* Stokowski also brought the sound of

Leading Ladies: Lady Day

Billie Holiday, also known as Lady Day, was always welcome in Philadelphia.

(Photo: William Gottlieb; via Wikimedia Commons, public domain)

ONE OF THE MOST FAMOUS MUSICIANS to come out of Philadelphia was the legendary Billie Holiday, also known as Lady Day. Although much of her life was spent in Baltimore and New York, Philadelphia welcomed her when New York clubs snubbed her because of her drug use.

From the beginning, Holiday faced numerous obstacles in her life. Her mother got pregnant out of wedlock and was kicked out of her house. She came to Philadelphia in 1915 to give birth to Holiday, whose birth name was Elinore Harris. Holiday's mom moved back to Baltimore to raise her daughter.

Holiday had a troubled youth and endured both physical and sexual abuse. Her mother moved to New York, and Holiday lived with her in a house of prostitution in Harlem.

From a young age, Holiday loved to sing and would often do so along with the records of blues legend Bessie Smith and jazz great Louis Armstrong. Holiday began singing in Harlem jazz clubs when she was a teenager, and at age 18 she was discovered by a producer named John Hammond. She had taken on the stage name of Billie Holiday at that point. Hammond helped her connect with up-and-coming jazz clarinetist Benny Goodman. Holiday went on to work with Duke Ellington, the Count Basie Orchestra, and Artie Shaw, becoming the first African American singer to work with a white orchestra.

But Holiday's adult life was as mired in turmoil as her youth. She had several marriages and became addicted to heroin. In 1947, her hotel room was raided and police arrested her on drug charges. She pleaded guilty after poor advice from her manager and ended up spending a year in a West Virginia women's detention center.

After her arrest, she lost her Cabaret Card, which all performers were required to have to work in New York clubs. Philadelphia, however, embraced her, and she often performed at the Showboat, which was a club in the basement of the Douglass Hotel, at Broad and Lombard Streets. She continued to battle addiction, however, and lost the fight in 1959 when she died from complications of alcohol and drug abuse.

Numerous musicians credit Billie Holiday with inspiration, including Frank Sinatra. Her sultry, emotional voice lives on in recordings, and in 2000 she was inducted into the Rock and Roll Hall of Fame.

the symphony to mainstream America by having concerts broadcasted and recorded. The "Grand Old Lady of Locust Street," a.k.a. the Academy of Music building, was ground zero for the orchestra's performances, recordings, and broadcasting. The stately Academy of Music is the oldest grand-opera house in the country that is still used for its original purpose. It currently hosts regular music performances from the Opera Company of Philadelphia, the Philly Pops with Peter Nero, and the Pennsylvania Ballet. Stokowski remained the leader of the Philadelphia Orchestra for nearly three decades and is widely considered both the father of the orchestra's "Philadelphia Sound" and one of the organization's greatest conductors.

PHILLY FACT Ulysses S. Grant received his nomination for his second term as president in the Academy of Music in 1872. Presidents Grover Cleveland and Richard Nixon also visited the Academy of Music.

Today the Sound of Philadelphia is a diverse one, with no one type of music dominating the scene. With several large concert venues, Philadelphia is often a stop for major artists of the day. And you can always count on hearing the sound of string bands on major holidays (see the sidebar on Mummers on page 131). Philadelphia hosts a huge concert on the Ben Franklin Parkway every year to celebrate Independence Day and has hosted a multiday concert in the same place called Made in America. The Sound of Philadelphia is alive and well.

CHAPTER 9

TAKE ME OUT TO THE BALLPARK

PHILADELPHIA IS A SPORTS TOWN. The city has five major professional sports teams, and fans who live and die by those teams. The city has produced Olympians, MVPs, and all-around champions, but it has also produced fans who could get so unruly that a temporary courtroom had to be established in a stadium to deal with their shenanigans. And in recent sports history, when a team has won a major playoff or championship, William Penn high atop City Hall dons some sports paraphernalia of the team to show his support.

From its early days, Philadelphia had a history of embracing sports. The first sporting event on record was a rowing competition along the Schuylkill River in 1732. Due to Philadelphia's placement along the Schuylkill and Delaware Rivers, rowing dominated early Philadelphia sports history, and to this day Philadelphia is home to major competitions where rowers take to the Schuylkill River along Boathouse Row to compete. For a time period around the Civil War, cricket was a popular and growing sport in Philadelphia, and several cricket clubs remain throughout the Delaware Valley. But the sport with the greatest longevity in the City of Brotherly Love is probably baseball. "Town ball," as baseball was originally called, came on the scene in the 1830s and has stuck around ever since.

America's Pastime

EARLY PHILADELPHIA CLUB TEAMS included the Olympics, organized in 1831, and the Athletics, created in 1859. Thousands of fans would show up to cheer on their favorite teams at a park located at Twenty-Fifth and Jefferson streets. The Athletics name would stick around for years and, although not affiliated, different teams would pop up throughout Philadelphia sports history with the same name. Within a few decades, the popularity of baseball took off across the country, and Philadelphia was no different. In 1865, Philadelphia's Athletics team signed the first professional baseball player, paying Alfred Reach $1,000 to sign a contract with the team. (Reach would later become the first owner of the Philadelphia Phillies.) And in 1871, teams banded together to form the National Association of Professional Base Ball Players. Major League Baseball, the current organizing body of professional baseball, doesn't recognize the National Association as the first professional baseball organization, however, due to issues with the organization's

PHILLY FACT Baseball player **Curt Flood** changed baseball history not for something he did in Philadelphia, but for something he *didn't* do. He was a center fielder for the St. Louis Cardinals when they tried to trade him to the Phillies in 1969. He didn't want to go, so he sued Major League Baseball, essentially creating the idea of free agency. His case went to the US Supreme Court, where he lost. But his case paved the way for future players to become free agents.

management and organization. MLB says it originated from the National League of Professional Baseball Clubs, which was created in 1876 and held its first official game in Philadelphia. On April 22, 1876, the Athletics and the Boston Red Caps, National League teams, took the field, with the Philadelphia team falling to Boston by one point.

Baseball teams came and went throughout the city's early days, but in 1883, the National League asked Reach to start a new team, which he called the Phillies. They played their first game on May 1 of that year at a park located at 24th Street and Ridge Avenue, but they had a dismal first season, ending with a record of 17-81. The Phillies have been with Philadelphia ever since, through good and bad times. And as the online Encyclopedia of Greater Philadelphia notes, the Phillies are "the oldest continuous one-name, one-city franchise in all of professional sports." In 2007, the Phillies marked their 10,000th loss, the first team to reach such a sad milestone. But the Phillies have had their day in the spotlight, too, winning World Series Championships in 1980 and 2008, much to the delight of Philadelphia fans. Many say that the team's win in 2008 effectively broke the curse of William Penn that had dominated Philadelphia professional sports teams for decades (see "The Curse of William Penn" on page 145).

The Philadelphia Athletics won the World Series in 1931.

(Photo: © abbasj812/Wikimedia Commons/ CC BY 2.0)

Pitch Perfect

IN 1901, the city welcomed the Philadelphia Athletics to the baseball scene as members of the newly formed American League. The team's leader was a former National League catcher and team manager named Cornelius McGillicuddy, better known as Connie Mack. Benjamin Shibe, Reach's sporting-goods business partner, invested in the Athletics as well. From the very beginning of the team's history, they would dominate the baseball scene not just in Philadelphia but across the country. While in Philadelphia, the team won the American League pennant nine times: 1902, 1905, 1910, 1911, 1913, 1914, 1929, 1930, and 1931. The team also claimed

Connie Mack (1862–1956) still holds the title of longest-serving manager in Major League Baseball.

(Photo: Paul Thompson; via Wikimedia Commons, public domain)

Shibe Park was home to both the Athletics and the Phillies.

(Photo: George Grantham Bain Collection, Library of Congress; via Wikimedia Commons, public domain)

world-champion status five times with World Series wins in 1910, 1911, 1913, 1929, and 1930.

While the Athletics brought Philadelphia its first World Series title, the team also ushered in another first for the city and the nation with the creation of its new baseball park. In 1909, Shibe Park, located at 21st and Lehigh Streets, became Major League Baseball's first ballpark made of concrete and steel. Tens of thousands of fans filled the stadium to watch the home team play, and often win. The park would celebrate another first 30 years later in May 1939, when it hosted the first night game ever played in the American League. Connie Mack still holds the title of longest-serving manager in the majors, and under his leadership, the A's won 3,776 games and lost 4,025, both records in their respective categories. Shibe Park was renamed Connie Mack Stadium in 1953. And the Phillies would also call the stadium home from 1887 to 1938.

Alas, the Athletics' time in Philadelphia came to an end in 1954 when the team moved to Kansas City. The team eventually moved to its current home in California in 1968 when the team became the Oakland Athletics. Shibe Park was demolished in 1976. Veterans Stadium was the Phillies' home from 1971 to 2003, when it met its demise via implosion. The Phillies now call Citizens Bank Park their home.

Racial Barriers

PHILADELPHIA WAS NOT QUICK to embrace an integrated sports environment, but the African American population wasn't going to miss out on the baseball craze. So they created their own league of teams that were incredibly popular. The first all-black teams formed in the 1860s, with one of the most popular teams led by civil rights leader Octavius Catto (see Chapter 5). He was a key figure in the integration of Philadelphia's streetcars, but in addition to his passion for equality, he had a passion for baseball. He helped create the Pythians, the city's second all-black baseball team, in 1867. Catto not only played second base and shortstop but also promoted, managed, and helped find funding for the team.

Catto tried to get the Pythians admitted to the National Association of Base Ball Players but was denied due to racial bias.

Catto's team made history, however, when the Pythians became the first all-black team to play against an all-white team. The Pythians were confident in their game and issued a challenge to white teams. The city's oldest team, the Olympics, accepted the challenge and played the first interracial game on record on September 3, 1869. The Olympics won the game 44–23, but the Pythians went on to play other white teams, and just a few weeks later they won against the all-white City Items. Sadly, the Pythians lost their leader in 1870 when Catto was assassinated on his way to vote in an election.

The Negro League teams continued to play through the early 1960s as Philadelphia was slow to integrate its baseball teams. Bob Trice became the first African American player for the Athletics in 1953. The Phillies signed their first black player in 1952, but the first African American player to make it out of the training season for the Phils and actually play for the team was John Kennedy in 1957.

Game Time

EVEN THOUGH BASEBALL CAME FIRST, other professional sports teams have been calling Philadelphia their home for decades. During football season, you can't go anywhere in the city without hearing fans chanting "E-A-G-L-E-S, **EAGLES!**" Fan support in the city waxes and wanes based on the wins and losses of each team. Philadelphia sports fans have earned a notorious reputation for being extreme lovers and haters of the hometown teams. But even if the home team is doing terribly, don't dare come to a game in Philadelphia wearing a rival team's paraphernalia if you know what's good for you. Philly fans will always, *always* stick up for the home team. In fact, you'd do well not to even wear rival-team logos while walking around the city. Yo, you got that? Don't say I didn't warn you.

Here's a breakdown of when each of our beloved teams came to the City of Brotherly Love.

■ **FOOTBALL** After baseball's domination in the sports scene in Philadelphia, professional football followed. A team called the Frankford Yellowjackets called the city home for a while, but folded in 1931. Two years later, the **Philadelphia Eagles** were born. Professional football really didn't want to have a team in Philadelphia, because there were blue laws on the books that forbade the playing of games on Sundays. A fellow named Bert Bell was a quarterback for the University of Pennsylvania's football team and wanted to start a pro team in Philadelphia. Bell rallied for support to allow Philadelphians to vote on whether or not they wanted to allow football to be played on Sundays. The legislature agreed, and the city's electorate voted to bring football to the city on Sundays. The Eagles played their first season in 1933 and finished in fourth place in the Eastern Division. The team can claim three National Football League Championships—in 1948, 1949, and 1960—before the creation of the Super Bowl, which the "Iggles" have yet to win.

■ **BASKETBALL** Professional basketball came to the city in 1946 when the Warriors arrived. They stayed in the city until 1962, before heading out west to California. It was 1963 when the **76ers** began calling Philadelphia their home. Prior to that, the team was located in Syracuse, New York, where they played under the name Nationals. Under the 76ers name, the team has won two National Basketball League Championships, one in 1967 led by Wilt Chamberlain, and one in 1983 led by Julius Erving and Moses Malone.

■ **HOCKEY** Philadelphia's first professional hockey team was called the Quakers. They played one season in the city in 1930–31, winning only four out of 44 games. In 1965, the National Hockey League decided it needed more teams. A year later, the city welcomed the **Philadelphia Flyers.** In the 1970s, the team got the nickname the "Broad Street Bullies," and they would go on to win back-to-back Stanley Cup titles in 1974 and 1975. Two legendary players during this era of the Flyers were Dave "The Hammer" Schultz and Bobby Clarke. Schultz still holds the NHL record for the most penalty minutes in a season, and Clarke was captain from 1973 to 1979 and was inducted to the Hockey Hall of Fame in 1987. Millions of Philadelphia fans came out for the parade to cheer on their Flyers. The Flyers have been in the playoffs since then, but they haven't taken the Stanley Cup since the era of the Broad Street Bullies.

- **SOCCER** The newest kid on the sports block is the **Philadelphia Union.** (Technically they don't play within the City of Philadelphia, but the franchise bears the city's name, so we'll include them.) The 16th team to join Major League Soccer, the Union was born on February 28, 2008. The team's home stadium is located in Chester, not too far outside of Philadelphia. "Union," by the way, is a nod to Philadelphia's status as the country's first capital city.

Sports Legends

PHILADELPHIA IS NO SLOUCH when it comes to sports legends. Here are a few superstars that the city's sports teams have been proud to call their own.

If you've ever been to Philadelphia, chances are you've driven along the beautiful Kelly Drive, which runs along the Schuylkill River. It's named for Olympic rower John B. Kelly, who won gold medals in both the single- and double-sculling events in the 1920 Olympics and then another gold in 1924. Plus, he was a six-time single-scull US National Champion. He was also well known as a local Democratic politician, a prominent businessman, and the father of actress-turned-princess Grace Kelly.

The 76ers produced several superstars over the team's history. The first player to be considered a legend was Wilt Chamberlain. A native son to Philadelphia, Chamberlain was born in 1936 and attended Overbrook High School. He played for the Warriors before joining the 76ers in 1965. Chamberlain was a record setter. Playing for the Warriors in 1962, he was the first player to ever score 100 points in a game. He helped the 76ers win the NBA Championship in 1967. Chamberlain was the first NBA player to score 30,000 career points. He died in 1999 in California but remains a Philadelphia sports legend. He was inducted into the Basketball Hall of Fame in 1978.

The winning 76ers team in 1983 produced two basketball legends: Julius "Dr. J" Erving and Moses Malone. Erving was born in 1950 in

The Curse of William Penn

WHETHER OR NOT YOU BELIEVE in superstitions, the Curse of Billy Penn is real. Or at least that's what some people think. Here's how the story goes.

There was a gentleman's agreement in place that no buildings in the city should be built taller than the top of William Penn's hat high atop City Hall. And builders abided by that agreement for decades.

Billy Penn kept watch over his city, and his spirit guided sports teams to victories. As mentioned in this chapter, the early 1980s saw both a World Series win and an NBA championship. But in 1987, Liberty Place popped up and rose above Penn's hat, which allegedly ticked him off something fierce. Soon other skyscrapers followed, and the city did not see a champion sports team for decades.

This little statue high atop the Comcast Building helped break the curse of Billy Penn.

(Photo: Dave Tavani)

Enter Comcast. The communications giant is headquartered in Philadelphia, and in 2007 it built a skyscraper taller than any other in the city. And they decided to put a tiny statue of William Penn at the top of the new building.

The Phillies won the World Series the next year, effectively breaking the curse.

Only you can decide if you believe in the curse, but Comcast isn't taking any chances. The company is planning on constructing a new, even taller building and is planning on making sure "Little Billy" stays on top of the city when it opens in 2017.

Leading Ladies: Philadelphia Freedom

ALTHOUGH MEN LARGELY DOMINATED the Philadelphia sports scene throughout its history, one legendary woman called Philadelphia her sports home for a short time.

Billie Jean King was an outstanding tennis player. She handily won numerous tennis championships including Wimbledon, the US Open, and the Australian Open. She helped create the Women's Tennis Association and fought for equal earnings for male and female tennis champs.

King is possibly most well known for a match against Bobby Riggs in 1973. Riggs was a Wimbledon champ himself and began challenging top female tennis players of the day. King agreed to play him in a match that became known as the "Battle of the Sexes," and she whooped Riggs easily before 50 million television viewers.

In 1974, King and her then-husband, Larry, founded the World Team Tennis coed league, with King joining as both a player and a coach of the Philadelphia Freedoms tennis team. King was the first woman coach of a professional tennis team that had both male and female players.

In the 1980s, King's personal life took center stage when a lawsuit outed her as gay and she became the first female sports superstar to openly embrace her homosexuality. She has since become a tireless advocate for LGBT rights.

King befriended singer Elton John in the 1970s. He was so taken with her that he decided to write a song in her honor. "Philadelphia Freedom" was released in 1975. It was a smash hit, can often be heard at Philadelphia sporting events, and has become somewhat of an anthem for the city.

New York, and Malone was born in 1955 in Virginia. The two worked together to bring home a Philadelphia win, the last NBA championship the basketball team has seen since. Erving was inducted into the Basketball Hall of Fame in 1993, and Malone was inducted in 2001.

Boxer Joe Frazier called Philadelphia home for much of his life. He was the world heavyweight-boxing champion from 1970 to 1973. Frazier was born in South Carolina but moved to Philadelphia as a teenager, where he worked in a slaughterhouse. He would often punch sides of beef for practice, which would later inspire Sylvester Stallone in his screen portrayal of Rocky Balboa. Frazier died of cancer in 2011 in Philadelphia.

The Phillies have many superstars to call their own, including the legendary Michael Jack Schmidt. Schmidt was born in Ohio and was a second-round pick from Ohio University in 1971. After making his debut with the Phillies in 1972, he became a 12-time All-Star player and joined an elite group of baseball players to hit more than 500 home runs in his career. He ended his career with a total of 548 homers. His primary position was third base. He helped the Phillies win the World Series in 1980 and was named the Most Valuable Player of that series. He was inducted into the National Baseball Hall of Fame in 1995.

When all is said and done, Philadelphians love their sports teams, for better or worse. And now that the Curse of Billy Penn is broken, the city can't wait for its next national-champion team.

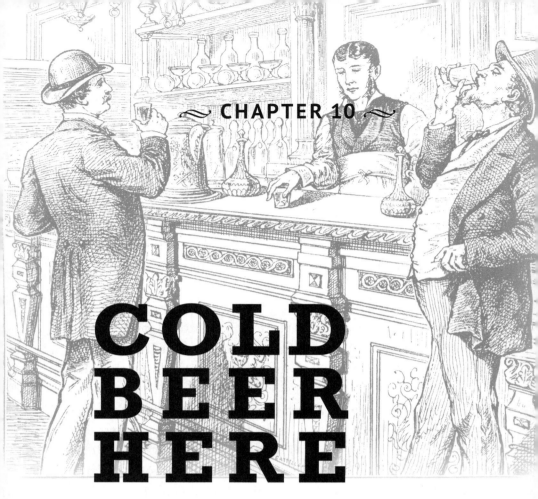

CHAPTER 10

COLD BEER HERE

Our DRINK has been Beer and Punch, made of Rum and Water: Our Beer was mostly made of Molasses, which well boyld, with Sassafras or Pine infused into it, makes very tolerable drink; but now they make Mault, and Mault Drink begins to be common, especially at the Ordinaries and the Houses of the more substantial People. In our great Town there is an able Man, that has set up a large Brew House, in order to furnish the People with good Drink, both there and up and down the River.

—William Penn, 1685

There cannot be good living where there is not good drinking.

—Benjamin Franklin, 1773

IF THERE'S ONE THING that Philadelphians have a lot of love for, it's an ice-cold brew. The city's history leads us to our lushness. Visitors to our great city also love to imbibe in what has been deemed one of the best beer-drinking cities in America, if not *the* best. In fact, beer has been beloved in Philadelphia since even before Penn set foot in his "greene countrie towne." But it's not just beer we love: It's fine wine and spirits, too.

While still in England and planning his Philadelphia, William Penn stated that he would not allow the establishment of taverns or alehouses in his city. Fortunately, he had a change of heart and decided before he left the Old Country that he would allow taverns, but there would be rules in place to regulate them so that they would become a positive influence on the city. When he first arrived in the city, Philadelphia's first tavern, the Blue Anchor, was established in 1681 at Front and Dock Streets, along Dock Creek. Legend has it that Penn sipped his first beer in his new city at the Blue Anchor. And, in fact, Penn liked beer enough to have his very own brew house built on his country estate, Pennsbury Manor.

> **PHILLY FACT** The **Man Full of Trouble Tavern** is the city's only surviving pre–Revolutionary War public house. Located at 127–29 Spruce St., it was built in 1760. It was open for historic tours for some years, but it closed to the public in 1994. **McGillin's Olde Ale House,** at 1310 Drury St., claims to be the city's oldest continuously operating tavern. It opened in 1860, and the drinks have been flowing ever since.

When Penn came, he also found that residents had already dug out caves along the Delaware River that had become watering holes. In fact, the city had a number of "public houses" in place where locals regularly imbibed alcoholic beverages that might have been made from pumpkins, cornstalks, or whatever else early Philadelphians could ferment and drink. By 1744, there were taverns everywhere in the city—at least 100 on record—and countless other illegal establishments. These public houses became places where people both openly discussed the politics of the day and celebrated a hard day's work. One such establishment was the City Tavern, built on Second Street between Walnut and Chestnut Streets. City Tavern was built in 1773 and was a favorite bar and restaurant for many of the founding fathers, including Ben

Franklin and George Washington. Members of both the First and Second Continental Congresses would meet there regularly to discuss politics while drinking and dining. Unfortunately, a fire destroyed part of the tavern, and the rest was taken down in 1856. However, just in time for the city's Bicentennial celebration, a replica of the original City Tavern was built in 1976 in its original location. City Tavern is still open for business, and diners can feast on Colonial-style food and drink while being served by staff in Colonial garb.

Philadelphia is believed to be the birthplace of porter-style beer in the New World. Porter is a dark, robust style of beer that is so named due to the popularity of the beverage among porters. Robert Hare was the son of a fellow who brewed porter beers in England. In 1774, Hare started a brewery in Northern Liberties and began making and selling his porter-style beer. Many historians credit Hare with being the first to brew porter in the Colonies.

Good Drink

ONCE THE BEER STARTED FLOWING, there was no stopping it. At the parade to celebrate the signing of the Constitution in 1787, several brewers participated, led by Reuben Haines, whom we read about briefly in Chapter 6. By 1793, Philadelphia was shipping more beer out of the city than any other seaport—more than all of them combined. Breweries were popping up everywhere, and a few families whom we've read about in other facets of society had a stake in the beer boom.

The popularity of ale beer came first. Some of the famous families involved in the early beer industry in the city were Haines, Morris, and Wister. Anthony Morris started his brewery in 1687 in today's Old City. His son, also named Anthony, eventually took over for Dad, and the brewery business was passed down for generations until 1836. At that point, a man named Francis Perot married a Morris, and the family continued to brew together for decades more.

In a city where you can walk into any bar, order a lager, and be handed a bottle or glass of Pennsylvania-brewed Yuengling, it's safe to say that we hold our lager very close to our hearts. It makes sense, then, that the first lager beer in America was brewed in our beloved metropolis. Historians think that the kind of yeast used to brew lager arrived in America in about the 1840s. A brewer named John Wagner, who was a Bavarian native, set up a tiny home brewery in Northern Liberties. He is widely credited with brewing America's first lager, and a historical marker now stands in the 800 block of North American Street to mark the occasion. Soon, lager brewing spread across the city as quickly as yeast devours sugar. In fact, a Brewer's Hall was even built for the city's centennial celebration.

As the population of the city continued to grow with the dawn of the Industrial Revolution, the need for "good drink" continued to grow. The city tried to make laws requiring drinking establishments to have a license. But nothing stopped Philadelphians from partaking in adult beverages, and by the early 19th century, the average Philadelphian drank nearly 10 gallons of liquor and more than 30 gallons of hard cider each year. The "Workshop of the World" was hard at work, and workers tossed back a cold one at the end of the workday. By midcentury, there were more than 900 legally operating taverns within the city.

In fact, a neighborhood developed in Philadelphia called Brewerytown, which is northwest of the art museum area, close to the Schuylkill River. The proximity of the river was key to the development of the neighborhood, in that the brewers had easy access to ice on the river, a necessity if you want to keep your beer cold. The area was largely undeveloped and served as the perfect place for breweries to dig cellars and ice houses. By the dawn of the 20th century, half of all the beer brewed in the city originated in Brewerytown.

After the Civil War, drinking beer and spirits was equated to being a social miscreant. Bosses also worried about their employees coming to work under the influence. Prohibition came in the early 1900s, and Philadelphians responded by getting their liquor and beer illegally. In 1923, police believed there were about 8,000 speakeasies in operation throughout the city. When Prohibition came to an end, Pennsylvania lawmakers decided it best to create laws to control alcohol licensing and distribution.

Philly Beer Week

PHILADELPHIANS LOVE THEIR BEER so much that they've created an annual event to celebrate all things beer. Philly Beer Week started in 2008, and even though the title might lead one to believe that the event is one week long, it's actually 10 days.

The festival kicks off with a massive beer-tasting event where the "Hammer of Glory" is used to tap the first keg at what is called the "Opening Tap." The Hammer travels around the city throughout the week and is often carried like an Olympic torch.

Philly Beer Week consists of beer-themed talks, tastings, and tours, as well as dinners and a lot of drinking. Always the trendsetter, Philadelphia has become a model for other cities, with more than 100 similar beer festivals popping up around the world.

How's that for proof that Philadelphia is indeed the best beer-drinking city in America?

Alas, the beer boom in the city didn't last for a variety of reasons. The Industrial Revolution was fizzling out big time throughout the city. Jobs were leaving, and so was the population. As the suburbs grew, the demand for good drink diminished. Breweries closed shop part-and-parcel throughout the decades, with the last remaining brewery, Schmidt's, closing its doors in the city in 1987. With Schmidt's departure, it was the first time in a 300-year span that Philadelphia was without breweries.

But fortunately for Philadelphia and all of its visitors, beer brewing in the city has made a significant comeback. Philadelphia currently hosts a number of breweries and brew pubs, and their numbers seem to grow every year, contributing to what is now seen as a craft-brew renaissance.

Probably the two biggest beer makers in the city, Yards Brewing Company and Philadelphia Brewing Company are important to this beer renaissance. In the 1990s, two college friends, Tom Kehoe and Jon Bovit, started Yards Brewing Company. Their beers were incredibly popular, allowing the company to grow and expand. Later in the decade, Nancy and Bill Barton began working for Yards

Yards Brewing Company helped remake Philadelphia as a beer-making city.

(Photo: © C. Smyth/Visit Philadelphia)

and invested in the company. In 2007, Kehoe and the Bartons parted ways, with Kehoe keeping the name and brands of Yards, and the Bartons keeping the brewery and all of the equipment. Philadelphia Brewing Company offered its first beer in 2008, a beer called Fleur de Lehigh, which was a tribute to Shibe Park. Yards and PBC are both wildly popular and continue to quench the thirst of Philadelphians and visitors daily.

Good Eats

WHILE WE PHILADELPHIANS are taking in a tipple, we love to have some tasty treats on hand. There are a few foods that are synonymous with Philadelphia: cheesesteaks, hoagies, soft pretzels, Tastykakes, and water ice (often pronounced "wooder ice"). And, of course, each food has a special connection to our beloved city.

Let's start with the beloved Philadelphia cheesesteak. The cheesesteak is essentially a steak sandwich—chopped chip steak on a long, Italian roll, usually served with fried onions and Cheez Whiz. The creator of the original Philadelphia cheesesteak was Harry Olivieri. The story goes that in 1930, Harry and his brother had a hot dog stand in South Philadelphia. But they got tired of eating their own hot dogs for lunch, so they cooked up a steak sandwich one day. The rest, as they say, is history. In 1940, the Olivieri brothers opened Pat's King of Steaks on Passyunk Avenue. Then in 1966, Joey Vento opened up Geno's, a competing cheesesteak shop directly across the street from Pat's. The two eateries light up Passyunk Avenue each night as locals and visitors come from across the city to get a cheesesteak fix. You could also pretty much get a cheesesteak anywhere in the city and the surrounding suburbs. Whose is the best? You'll have to see for yourself.

If you can't get a cheesesteak to feed your hunger, a hoagie is the next best thing. If you're not from Philadelphia, you might ask, "What's a hoagie?" It's essentially what the rest of the country refers to as a submarine sandwich, sub, hero, or grinder. Or, to get even more basic, it's lunchmeat on an Italian roll with lettuce, mayo or oil, tomatoes, and other fixin's. So why do we call them "hoagies?" There are a

Pat's and Geno's compete for the title of best cheesesteak.

(Photo: © Yuri Long/Wikimedia Commons/CC BY 2.0)

few theories, but the most plausible one is that a fellow by the name of Al DePalma opened up a sandwich shop and made these sub-type sandwiches. He called them "hoggies," intimating that one would have to be a hog to eat them. The word eventually morphed into "hoagies." In 1992, former Philadelphia Mayor Ed Rendell declared the hoagie the official sandwich of Philadelphia, which was most certainly embraced by local convenience-store chain, Wawa. Want to sound like a Philadelphian? Here's how to explain what you're doing for lunch today. "Yo, I'm heading to the Wawa to tap the MAC and grab a hoagie." Translation: "Hey. I'm going to the local convenience store to get some cash out at the ATM and buy a submarine sandwich."

The history of Philadelphia's obsession with soft pretzels and water ice is harder to trace, but most can agree that the Italian ice came to the city around the same time as a wave of Italian immigrants made the city their home. You can get Italian ice—essentially sugary, flavored, shaved ice—in other places in the country. But Philly is the only place you can get an authentic water ice. They are essentially the same thing, but we call ours by a different name. Either way, there's nothing quite so refreshing as a water ice on a steamy Philadelphia day.

Soft pretzels are the "anytime" food for Philadelphians. Missed breakfast? Grab a soft pretzel. Hosting a party? Get a tray of soft pretzels and you can't go wrong. The Philadelphia soft pretzel is not the heart-shaped pretzel you might see spinning on a rack under a heat lamp at a ballpark. Au contraire: The Philadelphia soft pretzel is more like a figure-eight and is served best warm and chewy, covered in salt, and doused with mustard. Like water ice, the pretzel gained popularity when German immigrants settled in the city.

If you grew up in or near the Philadelphia area, you can probably sing along to the jingle of the city's unofficial snack cake: "Nobody bakes a cake as tasty as a Tastykake." Tasty Baking Company was founded in 1914 in the Germantown section of the city and started out by selling full-size cakes. Within the first several months of operation, the company was selling millions of cakes. The company eventually started making snack-sized cakes that became a regular part of a

Tastykakes are an iconic Philadelphia snack.

(Photo: © M. Fischetti/Visit Philadelphia)

Philadelphian's lunch. The company grew so big that it moved to a bigger factory on Hunting Park Avenue, where it remained for decades. Popular variations include Chocolate Juniors, Butterscotch Krimpets, and the most popular, the Kandy Kake, a yellow cake covered with peanut butter and chocolate. Most recently, the company relocated to the Philadelphia Naval Business Center, and in 2011 Flowers Foods bought the Tasty Baking Company for $34 million.

∽ EPILOGUE ∽

A S OF THE WRITING OF THIS BOOK, Philadelphia is the fifth largest city in the country. The city has undergone some tough times and has seen extended periods of population loss. The collapse of the industrial economy ushered in many of those losses, because as jobs were lost, people went elsewhere to look for work. Murder and violence also increased, and there were periods of time where there seemed to be a general lack of safety across the city.

There is good news, however, for Penn's city. Philadelphia's population has been steadily increasing over the last few years, with the current population around 1.5 million. Demographically, today's Philadelphia is about 46 percent white and 44 percent black, with other races making up the remaining percentages.

Cities are like living, breathing beings. They are constantly on the move and constantly undergoing change. Much of Philadelphia, particularly the Center City area, has seen an amazing revitalization in the last few decades. There are more jobs, and the housing market is booming. Violent crimes are down, and the city is getting safer.

Yet there are still people who are struggling in this great city. The current poverty rate is 27 percent, and there seems to be a continuous wave of gentrification throughout many neighborhoods. As a city of neighborhoods, it is unsettling to longtime residents when their neighborhood starts to change its character. Some see gentrification as a revitalization, while others see it as a displacement of poor, mostly African American residents.

Philadelphia is a product of its past. If we look to all of the great things that have happened in the city over its lifetime thus far, history can repeat itself. Great things happen in a city when there is a love of innovation and a passion for growth. Even greater things can happen when there is love for each other and a common purpose: to make the city the best place to live for *everyone*—no exceptions.

The story of Philadelphia is indeed a love story, and we are only part of the way through its telling. I can't wait to read the next chapter.

∼ ACKNOWLEDGMENTS ∼

SO MANY PEOPLE HAVE HELPED ME in my journey to write this book. This book would not have been possible without my editor, Tim Jackson. From the book's inception, Tim has been a steady guide. I'm also forever grateful to the Master of Fine Arts in Creative Nonfiction program at Goucher College.

Thanks to my Wednesday-night writing buddy and dear friend, Patrick Rapa, for being a sounding board, a resource, and a creative genius. Thanks for all of your suggestions. Special thanks goes out to my number-one cheerleader and fellow Goucher Gopher, Carrie Hagen. Thanks for your constant support. Thanks to my daily support team: Jenn Miller, Tina Sullivan, Steve Kimball, and Kelly Shaak. Your friendships make the days easier. Shout-out to my soul sister Marnie Levinson; I cherish your friendship. Thanks to my neighbor Cathy Gilmore-Clough for helping me track down hard-to-find books. Every writer should have a librarian as a neighbor. Thanks also to the staff at the University of Pennsylvania's University Archives and Records Center. And thanks to everyone who offered suggestions for things to include in the book, particularly Jason Miller, who helped out with the sports chapter.

Thanks also to the folks at Visit Philadelphia, especially Courtney Smyth and Marisa Fischetti, who helped me track down some photos. Thanks to my husband, Dave, for his support, love, and respect of my writing space. Dave also gets a special acknowledgment for his awesome photos. Every writer should have such easy access to a great photographer. Special thanks to my mom and dad for giving me the freedom to find and fall in love with Philadelphia. Most of all, thanks to Clerisy Press for the opportunity to write this book about my beloved city.

159

~ BIBLIOGRAPHY ~

Avery, Ron. *A Concise History of Philadelphia.* Philadelphia: Otis Books, 1999.

Bishop, J. Leander, and Edwin T. Freedley. *A History of American Manufacturers from 1608 to 1860.* 1868. Reprint, Philadelphia: E. Young & Co., 1967.

Burt, Nathaniel. *The Perennial Philadelphians: the Anatomy of an American Aristocracy.* Boston: Little, Brown, 1963.

Encyclopedia of Greater Philadelphia. **philadelphiaencyclopedia.org.**

Glantz, Joseph. *Philadelphia Originals.* Atglen, PA: Schiffer Publishing, 2009.

Historical Society of Pennsylvania. **hsp.org.**

James, Edward T., Janet Wilson James, and Paul S. Boyer, eds. *Notable American Women.* Vol. 3, *1607–1950, P–Z.* Cambridge, MA: Harvard University Press, 1971.

Nash, Gary B. *Forging Freedom: The Formation of Philadelphia's Black Community, 1720–1840.* Cambridge, MA: Harvard University Press, 1988.

Simon, Roger D. *Philadelphia: A Brief History.* University Park, PA: Pennsylvania Historical Association, 2003.

Wagner, Rich, and Lew Bryson. *Philadelphia Beer: A Heady History of Brewing in the Cradle of Liberty.* Charleston, SC: History Press, 2012.

Uwishunu: The Official Tourism Blog of Philadelphia and the Countryside. **uwishunu.com.**

Weigley, Russell Frank. *Philadelphia: A 300 Year History.* New York: W. W. Norton, 1982.

∾ INDEX ∾

∼ ABOUT THE AUTHOR ∼

Photo: Dave Tavani

LORI LITCHMAN is a lifelong Pennsylvanian and has lived in Philadelphia long enough to consider herself a native. She holds an MFA in Creative Nonfiction from Goucher College. She lives and writes in the Germantown section of Philadelphia and spends many hours enjoying the beautiful space of Fairmount Park in Penn's "greene countrie towne." When she isn't writing, she's usually teaching English to nonnative speakers.